COURTS AND THE BODY POLITIC

Over the last half century, courts have come to play an increasingly expanded role in democracies. That role is studied by historians, political scientists, constitutional lawyers and political theorists, but it is also important to all who are concerned about the practice and future of democracy. This book explores why it is that courts are playing this expanded role and examines two of the most distinctive features of their role: their relationship with the executive arm of government and their part in protecting fundamental rights. The book argues that the role played by courts in modern democracies varies across time and place and depends on a range of factors including constitutional text, constitutional history and legal and political culture. This book draws on Justice O'Regan's experience as a judge of South Africa's Constitutional Court.

JUSTICE KATE O'REGAN served as one of the first eleven judges of South Africa's Constitutional Court, which was established shortly after the transition to democracy in 1994. Her fifteen-year term ran from 1994 to 2009. Since her term on the court ended, she has served as an ad hoc judge of the Namibian Supreme Court (2010–2016) and as Chairperson of the United Nations Internal Justice Council (2008–2012), as well as serving as a judge on several international tribunals. Since 2016, she has been Professor of Human Rights Law and inaugural Director of the Bonavero Institute of Human Rights in the Faculty of Law at the University of Oxford.

THE HAMLYN LECTURES

COURTS AND THE BODY POLITIC

KATE O'REGAN
University of Oxford

CAMBRIDGE
UNIVERSITY PRESS

CAMBRIDGE
UNIVERSITY PRESS

Shaftesbury Road, Cambridge CB2 8EA, United Kingdom

One Liberty Plaza, 20th Floor, New York, NY 10006, USA

477 Williamstown Road, Port Melbourne, VIC 3207, Australia

314–321, 3rd Floor, Plot 3, Splendor Forum, Jasola District Centre,
New Delhi – 110025, India

103 Penang Road, #05–06/07, Visioncrest Commercial, Singapore 238467

Cambridge University Press is part of Cambridge University Press & Assessment, a department of the University of Cambridge.

We share the University's mission to contribute to society through the pursuit of education, learning and research at the highest international levels of excellence.

www.cambridge.org
Information on this title: www.cambridge.org/9781009545792

DOI: 10.1017/9781009545808

When citing this work, please include a reference to the DOI 10.1017/9781009545808

First published 2025

A catalogue record for this publication is available from the British Library

A Cataloging-in-Publication data record for this book is available from the Library of Congress

ISBN 978-1-009-54579-2 Hardback

To Alec, with love and gratitude

CONTENTS

The Hamlyn Trust *page* viii

The Hamlyn Lectures xi

Acknowledgements xvi

1 The Expanding Role of Courts in Modern Constitutions 1

2 Courts and the Executive Branch 37

3 Courts and Human Rights 73

Select Bibliography 113

Index 123

THE HAMLYN TRUST

The Hamlyn Trust owes its existence today to the will of the late Miss Emma Warburton Hamlyn of Torquay, who died in 1941 at the age of eighty. She came of an old and well-known Devon family. Her father, William Bussell Hamlyn, practised in Torquay as a solicitor and JP for many years, and it seems likely that Miss Hamlyn founded the trust in his memory. Emma Hamlyn was a woman of strong character, intelligent and cultured; well-versed in literature, music and art; and a lover of her country. She travelled extensively in Europe and Egypt, and apparently took considerable interest in the law and ethnology of the countries and cultures that she visited. An account of Miss Hamlyn by Professor Chantal Stebbings of the University of Exeter may be found, under the title 'The Hamlyn Legacy', in Volume 42 of the published lectures.

Miss Hamlyn bequeathed the residue of her estate on trust in terms which, it seems, were her own. The wording was thought to be vague, and the will was taken to the Chancery Division of the High Court, which in November 1948 approved a Scheme for the administration of the trust. Paragraph 3 of the Scheme, which follows Miss Hamlyn's own wording, is as follows:

> The object of the charity is the furtherance by lectures or otherwise among the Common People of the United Kingdom of Great Britain and Northern Ireland of the

> knowledge of the Comparative Jurisprudence and Ethnology of the Chief European countries including the United Kingdom, and the circumstances of the growth of such jurisprudence to the Intent that the Common People of the United Kingdom may realise the privileges which in law and custom they enjoy in comparison with other European Peoples and realising and appreciating such privileges may recognise the responsibilities and obligations attaching to them.

The Trustees are to include the vice-chancellor of the University of Exeter; representatives of the Universities of London, Leeds, Glasgow, Belfast and Wales; and persons co-opted. At present there are eight Trustees.

From the outset it was decided that the objects of the Trust could be best achieved by means of an annual course of public lectures of outstanding interest and quality by eminent lecturers, and by their subsequent publication and distribution to a wider audience. The first of the Lectures were delivered by the Rt Hon. Lord Justice Denning (as he then was) in 1949. Since then there has been an unbroken series of annual

Lectures published until 2005 by Sweet & Maxwell and from 2006 by Cambridge University Press. A complete list of the Lectures may be found on pages xi to xv. In 2005 the Trustees decided to supplement the Lectures with an annual Hamlyn Seminar, normally held at the Institute of Advanced Legal Studies in the University of London, to mark the publication of the Lectures in printed book form. The Trustees have also, from time to time, provided financial support for a variety of projects which, in various ways, have disseminated knowledge or have promoted to a wider public understanding of the law.

This, the seventy fourth series of lectures, was delivered by Kate O'Regan at the Queen's University of Belfast, the University of Glasgow and the Bonavero Institute of Human Rights at the University of Oxford. The Board of Trustees would like to record its appreciation to Kate O'Regan and also the three venues which generously hosted these Lectures.

AVROM SHERR
Chair of the Trustees

THE HAMLYN LECTURES

1949 Freedom under the Law by the Rt Hon. Lord Denning
1950 The Inheritance of the Common Law by Richard O'Sullivan
1951 The Rational Strength of English Law by Professor F. H. Lawson
1952 English Law and the Moral Law by Professor A. L. Goodhart
1953 The Queen's Peace by Sir Carleton Kemp Allen
1954 Executive Discretion and Judicial Control by Professor C. J. Hamson
1955 The Proof of Guilt by Professor Glanville Williams
1956 Trial by Jury by the Rt Hon. Lord Devlin
1957 Protection from Power under English Law by the Rt Hon. Lord MacDermott
1958 The Sanctity of Contracts in English Law by Professor Sir David Hughes Parry
1959 Judge and Jurist in the Reign of Victoria by C. H. S. Fifoot
1960 The Common Law in India by M. C. Setalvad
1961 British Justice: The Scottish Contribution by Professor Sir Thomas Smith
1962 Lawyer and Litigant in England by the Rt Hon. Sir Robert Megarry

1963 Crime and the Criminal Law by the Baroness Wootton of Abinger

1964 Law and Lawyers in the United States by Dean Erwin N. Griswold

1965 New Law for a New World? by the Rt Hon. Lord Tangley

1966 Other People's Law by the Rt Hon. Lord Kilbrandon

1967 The Contribution of English Law to South African Law: and the Rule of Law in South Africa by the Hon. O. D. Schreiner

1968 Justice in the Welfare State by Professor H. Street

1969 The British Tradition in Canadian Law by the Hon. Bora Laskin

1970 The English Judge by Henry Cecil

1971 Punishment, Prison and the Public by Professor Sir Rupert Cross

1972 Labour and the Law by Professor Sir Otto Kahn-Freund

1973 Maladministration and its Remedies by Sir Kenneth Wheare

1974 English Law – the New Dimension by the Rt Hon. Lord Scarman

1975 The Land and the Development; or, The Turmoil and the Torment by Sir Desmond Heap

1976 The National Insurance Commissioners by Sir Robert Micklethwait

1977 The European Communities and the Rule of Law by Lord Mackenzie Stuart

1978 Liberty, Law and Justice by Professor Sir Norman Anderson
1979 Social History and Law Reform by Professor Lord McGregor of Durris
1980 Constitutional Fundamentals by Professor Sir William Wade
1981 Intolerable Inquisition? Reflections on the Law of Tax by Hubert Monroe
1982 The Quest for Security: Employees, Tenants, Wives by Professor Tony Honoré
1983 Hamlyn Revisited: The British Legal System Today by Lord Hailsham of St Marylebone
1984 The Development of Consumer Law and Policy – Bold Spirits and Timorous Souls by Sir Gordon Borrie
1985 Law and Order by Professor Ralf Dahrendorf
1986 The Fabric of English Civil Justice by Sir Jack Jacob
1987 Pragmatism and Theory in English Law by Professor P. S. Atiyah
1988 Justification and Excuse in the Criminal Law by Professor J. C. Smith
1989 Protection of the Public – A New Challenge by the Rt Hon. Lord Justice Woolf
1990 The United Kingdom and Human Rights by Dr Claire Palley
1991 Introducing a European Legal Order by Gordon Slynn
1992 Speech and Respect by Professor Richard Abel

1993 The Administration of Justice by Lord Mackay of Clashfern

1994 Blackstone's Tower: The English Law School by Professor William Twining

1995 From the Test Tube to the Coffin: Choice and Regulation in Private Life by the Hon. Mrs Justice Hale

1996 Turning Points of the Common law by the Rt Hon. the Lord Cooke of Thorndon

1997 Commercial Law in the Next Millennium by Professor Roy Goode

1998 Freedom, Law and Justice by the Rt Hon. Lord Justice Sedley

1999 The State of Justice by Professor Michael Zander QC

2000 Does the United Kingdom still have a Constitution? by Professor Anthony King

2001 Human Rights, Serious Crime and Criminal Procedure by Professor Andrew Ashworth QC

2002 Legal Conundrums in our Brave New World by Baroness Kennedy of the Shaws

2003 Judicial Activism by the Hon. Justice Michael Kirby AC CMG

2004 Rights at Work: Global, European and British Perspectives by Sir Bob Hepple QC, FBA

2005 Can Human Rights Survive? by Professor Conor Gearty

2006 The Sovereignty of Law: The European Way by Sir Francis Jacobs KCMG, QC

2007	The Prisoners' Dilemma by Professor Nicola Lacey
2008	Judging Civil Justice by Dame Hazel Genn
2009	Widening Horizons: The Influence of Comparative Law and International Law on Domestic Law by Lord Bingham
2010	Lawyers and the Public Good: Democracy in Action? by Alan Paterson
2011	The Rule of Law and the Measure of Property by Jeremy Waldron
2012	Aspects of Law Reform: An Insider's Perspective by Jack Straw
2013	The Common Law Constitution by Sir John Laws
2014	UK, EU and Global Administrative Law by Paul Craig
2015	A "Magna Carta" for Children? – Rethinking Children's Rights by Professor Michael Freeman
2016	Fairness in Criminal Justice: Golden Threads and Pragmatic Patches by Dame Sian Elias
2017	Thinking about Statutes: Interpretation, Interaction, Improvement by Professor Andrew Burrows QC
2018	Making Comparisons in Equality Law by Robin Allen
2019	English Law under Two Elizabeths by Sir John Baker
2020	The Great Experiment: Constructing a European Union under the Rule of Law from a Group of Diverse Sovereign States by Eleanor Sharpston QC
2021	Advocacy by Lord Pannick QC
2022	Courts and the Body Politic by Professor Catherine O'Regan

ACKNOWLEDGEMENTS

There are many to thank for their support and assistance during the writing and delivery of these lectures. Firstly, I would like to thank the trustees of the Hamlyn Trust for placing their faith in me to deliver the 2022 lectures. As only the fourth South African, by my count, to deliver these lectures and to follow Judge Oliver Schreiner, Professor Tony Honoré and Sir Bob Hepple, all eminent and principled South African jurists who I have admired since I was a law student, was simultaneously a signal honour and a daunting prospect. I am especially indebted to Professor Avrom Sherr, who attended all the lectures and was an engaging companion and interlocutor throughout. Secondly, I would like to thank colleagues and friends who read early versions of the lectures, especially Professor Nick Barber, Professor Aileen Kavanagh and Professor Tarunabh Khaitan. Their insights greatly improved the lectures, while any errors of course remain mine. Thirdly, I would like to thank colleagues at Queens' University Belfast and the University of Glasgow who hosted the lectures. It was a privilege to be able to speak at both universities, and their generous hospitality and kindness is deeply appreciated. I also thank my colleagues at the Bonavero Institute of Human Rights in the Faculty of Law at the University of Oxford, my home institution, where the third lecture was delivered. Fourthly, I thank Lauren Schaefer who ably assisted with the preparation of the lectures for publication. Fifthly, I would like to thank Tobias Ginsberg and the team at Cambridge University Press for their patience and support during the publication process. And finally, I would like to thank my husband, Alec Freund, who was a steadfast supporter during both the writing and delivery of the lectures, as he has been throughout my rather surprising career. Many of the ideas contained in the lectures have been developed over a lifetime of lively conversations with Alec, and I am deeply grateful to him for his unwavering loyalty and loving support over many years.

1

The Expanding Role of Courts in Modern Constitutions

Belfast, 2 November 2022

Introduction

On a cool spring morning in October 1994, when the jacarandas were in full flower in Johannesburg, the judges of South Africa's new Constitutional Court met for the first time. The constitutional text made it plain that the court was to be a powerful court. The court was conferred with a novel jurisdiction to determine whether the constitution to be drafted by the newly elected parliament sitting as a constitutional assembly complied with the constitutional principles that had been agreed by the former National Party government, the liberation movements and other political parties during the negotiated transition from apartheid to democracy. It also had a constitutional duty to declare invalid any legislation, or conduct of the President or Parliament, that it found to be inconsistent with the Constitution.

At that first meeting, our agenda was long and extraordinary and included

- Developing rules to regulate how cases would be brought and heard by the court. We discussed whether we should permit the admission of amici curiae or intervenors in proceedings (deciding yes), whether parties should be allowed to settle cases that had been brought to the court without court permission (deciding no), in what languages cases could be filed and heard (deciding in any of the country's eleven official languages).

- Planning the layout of the new court room and building (the court was temporarily housed in a rather plain, modern office building just north of the city that had not been built to house a court and had no court room). Planning the court's layout required us to think about the court's iconography (its logo or seal and the decoration of its public and private spaces). We rejected the traditional scales of justice as a seal for the court and opted instead for a woodcut image of a tree, under which people were sheltering, thus drawing on the African tradition of public hearings conducted under trees.
- Planning other aspects of the court's public persona – modes of dress (should we wear gowns and if so in what colour and style, deciding we should wear gowns and opting for non-traditional deep green (one of the colours in the new flag)); and modes of address (should we adopt the traditional modes inherited from colonial past – His Lordship Mr xxx – or should we abandon them, deciding to abandon them and opting instead for the simple Judge or Justice xx).
- We also needed to decide how we would work together – eleven judges drawn from very different backgrounds, as the Constitution mandated (seven of the judges were white and four black, nine male and two female). Should we have a system of seniority amongst us as most senior courts do, depending on leadership status and the date of

> appointment to the court – a status that in some courts confers benefits such as the allocation of chambers amongst the judges, the allocation of judgment-writing responsibilities, seating in the court chamber and even in the private conference room? (We opted for no system of seniority, save for the presiding judge, now the chief justice and the deputy chief justice). Other questions about the internal working of the court included whether judges should have law clerks, and if so how to appoint them (we decided yes, with judges appointing their own clerks) and whether judgments should be published on the internet (a novel idea at the time), and if so whether we should use paragraph numbers in our judgments (deciding yes, but with some colleagues reluctant, thinking that paragraph numbers would wreck their judicial prose and interrupt the flow of judgments).

The items on the agenda were intensely practical and urgent: the court needed to get up and running. Cases were accumulating on its roll and the plan was to hear our first cases just three months later in February. Yet at the time we met, we did not yet have a functional court room and only a skeleton staff.

But our agenda also raised questions of profound institutional and constitutional significance. What does it mean to be a constitutional court in a state in transition from a racist, unequal and authoritarian past to a democratic and (hopefully) more egalitarian future? How should the court engage with longstanding legal traditions and practices? What should the court's relationship be not only with the other arms of government, the newly elected democratic Parliament and President

Mandela (who had appointed the judges) and with existing courts, but also with South African society more broadly and other key institutions of the body politic, such as the press, the legal profession, civil society, political parties and universities?

These questions were directed at three things: first, the functioning of the court in adjudicating cases and producing judgments (its primary public function); second, the public persona of the court in relation to other organs of the body politic, that is, its values and identity in the body politic, which would at least in part define its relationship with the executive, the legislature, provincial governments and municipalities, other constitutional agencies, such as the prosecution agency and independent accountability mechanisms, civil society, political parties, the broader legal community (other courts, practising lawyers and legal academy) and the media; and third, the internal working relationships, practices and culture within the court.

The five days the court spent debating, and answering these questions, were of fundamental importance for the development of the court. In a sense, that week in Johannesburg the Constitutional Court was 'inventing itself and its tradition'. Law, as Martin Krygier has observed, is 'a profoundly traditional social practice, and it must be'.[1] Participating in such a tradition, Krygier argues,

> involves sharing a way of speaking about the world which . . . shapes, forms and in part envelops the thought

[1] Martin Krygier, 'Law as Tradition' (1986) 5 *Law and Philosophy* 237–262, 239.

> of those who speak it and think through it. . . . It moulds the thinking of insiders even where . . . they least realise and evades the grasp of outsiders determined to pin it down. Of course, where legal traditions are weak, or where the traditions of law are overwhelmed by the imperatives of power, particularly dictatorial power, 'law' . . . may simply be a malleable instrument of power-wielders.[2]

If law is, in this sense, a tradition, it should not be surprising that its institutions also self-consciously engage with both establishing and maintaining that tradition. It is not surprising either that a newly established court with a powerful public role should think about its institutional traditions. For Hobsbawm, invented tradition is 'a set of practices, normally governed by overtly or tacitly accepted rules and of a ritual or symbolic nature, which seek to inculcate certain values and norms of behaviour by repetition, which automatically implies continuity with the past'.[3] Hobsbawm notes that one of the three main types of invented traditions are those that arise when 'establishing or legitimizing institutions, status or relations of authority',[4] as the Constitutional Court was doing. He goes on to note that those revolutionary or

[2] Ibid., 244.

[3] Eric Hobsbawm, 'Introduction' in Eric Hobsbawm and Terence Ranger (eds.), *The Invention of Tradition* (Cambridge University Press, 2012, first published 1983), 1.

[4] Ibid., 9. The other two types are: those traditions establishing social cohesion or the membership of groups, real or artificial communities; and those whose purpose is socialisation, the inculcation of beliefs, value systems and conventions of behaviour.

progressive moments that break with the past have 'their own relevant past' to which they may refer.

The judges of the Constitutional Court thought about these questions, recognising that the court's public persona had to signal its institutional values, role and identity. And that the court's persona needed to signal that the court sought both to retain elements of the legal tradition of the past while simultaneously making a fundamental break with elements of the past that were authoritarian and racist. Ismail Mahomed, the deputy president of the court and subsequently chief justice, articulated this understanding in one of the first judgments of the court, in one of the most cited passages in all of the court's jurisprudence: 'The South African Constitution ... retains from the past only what is defensible and represents a decisive break from, and a ringing rejection of, that part of the past which is disgracefully racist, authoritarian, insular, and repressive'.[5] This was a delicate balance to achieve, both in the court's jurisprudence and practice, and in its representation of itself in the broader body politic. In concluding his study of invented traditions, Hobsbawm notes that 'conscious invention succeeded mainly in proportion to its success in broadcasting on a wavelength to which the public was ready to tune in'.[6]

But although those days felt momentous for the court, they were by no means unique. Since 1945, an explosion of constitution-making around the world has resulted in the establishment of courts with important constitutional powers. The structure and text of constitutions often requires

[5] *S v Makwanyane and Others* [1995] ZACC 3, para. 262.
[6] Hobsbawm, n. 3, 263.

a mechanism for the resolution of disputes: for example, disputes between federal and regional or local governments about their relative powers, disputes about the lawfulness of the exercise of executive and administrative powers, and of course, importantly, disputes about the rights of members of the public. Sometimes these have been brand new constitutions, as in the case of many postcolonial countries across Africa and Asia; sometimes they have been introduced after a period of military rule as in many countries in Latin America and Africa; and sometimes they have resulted from piecemeal constitutional developments, such as the Good Friday peace process in Northern Ireland or the patriation of the Canadian Constitution in the mid-1980s.

This book argues that the spread of constitutionalism since the eighteenth century, and more rapidly since the end of the Second World War, has been a major driver of the new roles that courts have come to play across the globe. The precise contours of the role of courts vary across constitutional systems, not only because of constitutional text but also because of historical, social, economic and political circumstances and, importantly, because of political and legal culture.

Most of the current debates about courts have been developed in the light of the experience of courts in only a handful of countries of the global north. In particular, much of the current scholarship and commentary about the role of courts in democracies is heavily influenced by the experience and traditions of the United States. There the key debate concerns the so-called counter-majoritarian dilemma: can it be consistent with democratic principles for a small handful of unelected judges to decide the key political issues of the day, particularly given a constitutional text which provides scant guidance as to how those decisions should be made? The deep political and social polarisation in the United States and the current ideological composition of the US Supreme Court spectacularly on view in the decisions rendered at the end of its term in June 2022 when it reversed *Roe v Wade*[7] and restricted the New York state's ability to introduce gun control measures (decisions which seem not to have popular support across the United States), mean that this debate is likely to intensify in the years ahead. It is, of course, an important debate, but it is one which arises within a particular society with a distinctive legal culture and a constitution that is almost impossible to amend and that is over two centuries old.

But there are other sceptical views about the role of courts in modern constitutional democracies. Take Martin Loughlin's argument in his recent book, *Against Constitutionalism*, for example.[8] Using examples from many parts of the world, though with a particular focus on the United States, United Kingdom and Germany, Loughlin argues that the key characteristics of modern constitutionalism lie in a written constitution that is the basic or fundamental law of a polity, supervised by inevitably powerful courts, and which provides a comprehensive and permanent scheme of government, based on the principle of representative government and the separation of powers.[9]

[7] 410 US 113 (1973).

[8] Martin Loughlin, *Against Constitutionalism* (Harvard University Press, 2022).

[9] Ibid., 6.

The problem with constitutionalism so defined, Loughlin suggests, is that it gets in the way of democracy.[10] Directing civic energies towards courts rather than politics weakens parties and legislatures, and often results in centring individualism rather than collective action. It also provides no bulwark, indeed may instead be a trojan horse, he suggests, for what he calls ordo-constitutionalism, whose 'mantra is the "free economy and the strong state"'[11] and which thus imposes a particular vision of the relationships between government and economy, between public and private, and between state and society. Ordo-constitutionalism fits well, he argues with a particular view of the global neoliberal economic order, which amongst other things privileges free movement of capital, but not of labour, and safeguards property and free trade against protectionist or redistributive policies.[12]

These critical views of courts and constitutionalism are often expressed as general claims that apply in every setting. A key purpose of this book is to destabilise such ambitious claims, by asserting that the role courts play in societies across the contemporary world varies widely and is dependent not only on constitutional text but also on history, politics and culture. Firm and general normative claims about whether what courts do is good or bad may founder when examined in the context of particular societies. The book will

[10] A similar argument is made by Jeremy Waldron in *Political Political Theory* (Harvard University Press2016), especially ch. 9, 'The Core of the Case against Judicial Review', 198.

[11] Loughlin, n. 8. [12] See ibid., 186.

seek to broaden our gaze beyond the countries of the global north, an ambition I think that could be said at least partly to be in accord with Miss Hamlyn's testamentary instructions for the Hamlyn Lectures.[13] It will be an exercise in comparative constitutional law and jurisprudence, although it will extend beyond the 'Chief European countries' that she specified in her will.

One final point needs to be made before outlining the rest of this chapter. And that is to talk a little about the state of democracy in our times. With the fall of the Berlin Wall in 1989, Francis Fukuyama famously pondered whether we may be witnessing 'the end of history', 'that is, the end point of mankind's ideological evolution and the universalisation of Western liberal democracy as the final form of human government'.[14] Although in the years immediately after the fall of the Berlin Wall, many countries made the transition from authoritarianism to democracy, forming part of what Samuel

[13] Miss Hamlyn's will established the lectures with the following instructions:

> Upon trust to apply the income of the Trust Fund in the furtherance by lectures or otherwise among the Common People of this Country of the knowledge of the Comparative Jurisprudence and the Ethnology of the Chief European countries including our own and the circumstances of the growth of such Jurisprudence to the intent that the Common People of our Country may realise the privileges which in law and custom they enjoy in comparison with other European Peoples and realising and appreciating such privileges may recognize the responsibilities and obligations attaching to them.

[14] See Francis Fukuyama, 'The End of History?' (1989) 16 *The National Interest* 3–18, 4.

Huntington famously called the third wave of democratisation,[15] the progress towards democratisation has slowed and indeed reversed. In its latest 2022 report *Freedom in the World*, Freedom House reports the sixteenth year of democratic decline, titling its report 'The Global Expansion of Authoritarian Rule'. This decline has been variously called democratic backsliding, democratic recession, or democratic decay.[16]

Unlike the democratic decline before 1990, democracy's current decline is rarely the result of a classic coup d'état: indeed, the number of coups d'état has declined sharply.[17] One of the key characteristics of modern democratic decline is what Nancy Bermeo calls executive aggrandisement,[18] in which the executive branch of the government weakens institutional checks on its exercise of power, often hampering the ability of opposition parties to challenge its preferences. The undermining of these institutional checks is often achieved through legal and constitutional means. Media freedoms, judicial independence and civil society organisations have been the subject of constraints in different ways. Another

[15] See Samuel Huntington, *The Third Wave: Democratisation in the Late Twentieth Century* (University of Oklahoma, 1993).

[16] See, for example, Larry Diamond, 'Facing Up to the Democratic Recession' (2015) 26 *Journal of Democracy* 141; Tom Ginsburg and Aziz Huq, *How to Save a Constitutional Democracy* (University of Chicago Press, 2018); Steven Levitsky and Daniel Ziblatt, *How Democracies Die: What History Reveals about Our Future* (Penguin, 2018).

[17] See Nancy Bermeo, 'On Democratic Backsliding' (2016) 27 *Journal of Democracy* 4–19. See also Tom Ginsburg and Aziz Huq, 'How to Lose a Constitutional Democracy' (2018) 65 *University of California Law Review* 78.

[18] Bermeo, n. 17, 10.

characteristic of democratic backsliding according to Bermeo is strategic manipulation of elections to favour incumbents.[19]

Democratic decline is also happening at the same time as the reassertion of the legitimacy of authoritarian modes of government, particularly by China and Russia. Fukuyama's speculation that 'ideological evolution' had ended in 1989 and liberal democracy had become the final form of government we can now see was clearly wrong. And the consequence is that, across the world, the questions on how to protect human freedom and flourishing, and ensure that governments act in an accountable manner remain as starkly pertinent today as they have at any time in the last few hundred years.

I turn now to the structure of this chapter. I am going to first explain the phrase 'the body politic' in the title of this book, and why I think it helps understand something important about courts as institutions in a broader system of governance. Then, I am going to discuss the risks and benefits of looking across global experience to explore and understand the role of courts beyond one jurisdiction. Next, the chapter will explore the rise of written constitutions, outlining the challenging circumstances in which most modern constitutions are made (or amended) and describing some of the key roles that courts now play in modern constitutional frameworks. Finally, I will argue that the expanded role of courts arises from the challenge of building functional political communities, which is the goal of most constitution-making. Whether courts perform their expanded roles well, I will

[19] Ibid., 13.

suggest, depends not only on the courts themselves but also on the broader body politic.

The Body Politic

The metaphor of the 'the body politic' has a long genealogy, stretching back to Aristotle, where in Book Three of the *Politics*, he speaks of the consequence of many people coming together in a political community to exercise authority in the following well-known passage:

> For each individual among the many has a share of excellence and practical wisdom, just as they become, in a manner, one man who has many pairs of feet and hands and many senses, so also do they become one in regard to character and thought.[20]

The metaphor of the body politic was extensively used in republican Rome, where it was built on a founding fable of the republic that is recounted by many sources.[21] In the early years of the republic, the Roman *plebs* abandoned the city to protest against the senate. One of the senators was sent to speak to the *plebs* to persuade them to return to the city. In his speech to the *plebs*, the senator explained that a state is like a

[20] Aristotle, *Politics*, Book 3, 1281b [1]. See also Sophie Smith, 'Democracy and the Body Politic from Aristotle to Hobbes' (2018) 46 *Political Theory* 167–196, 175.

[21] See, for example, Titus Livius (Livy), Book 2, *History of Rome*, ch. 32 and the full analysis of sources in Brian Walters, *The Deaths of the Republic: Imagery of the Body Politic in Ciceronian Rome* (Oxford University Press, 2020), ch. 1.

human body, both consisting of many parts, none of which has the same function or performs the same service as any other, yet each contributes to the common good and receives essential benefits in return, which are distributed in a manner beneficial to all.

The senator then told the fable (which indeed is included in Aesop's collection) of how in a previous time the parts of the body had been in conflict, particularly with the stomach who, the other parts of the body said, benefited from their work, yet did not give them anything in return; so they conspired to deprive the stomach of food. When the body began to waste away, the other body parts realised the important role played by the stomach. According to the authors, by telling this fable, the senator persuaded the *plebs* to return to the city.[22]

This founding fable was invoked by many Roman politicians and writers of later centuries, often as a prelude to the diagnosis of a contemporary illness of the Roman body politic. The implicit messages of the metaphor in Roman times were the interdependence of Rome's individual limbs and body parts, and the importance of cooperation between them, for Rome to flourish. Brian Walters observes that 'nearly every instance [of the use of the metaphor of the body politic] is to inspire a particular course of action. In every case the imagery's evocative persuasiveness is key'.[23]

The metaphor survived into medieval times, where many authors used it. John of Salisbury, for example, used it in his work *Policraticus,* in which he argued that 'a

[22] See Walters, n. 21, 10. [23] Ibid., 10.

well-organised political community will resemble a healthy human body, guided by the soul (priesthood), ruled by a wise head (the king) and populated by all the limbs and organs (from the counselling heart to the peasant feet) necessary for the efficient, just and mutually beneficial functioning of the entire organism'.[24] And the metaphor is to be found as well in the writings of the renaissance political philosophers such as Machiavelli and Thomas Hobbes. And even today, the metaphor appears quite regularly in contemporary political discourse, although not always in high intellectual debate. Boris Johnson, for example, described himself in 2005 as 'a mere toenail in the body politic', an assessment with which some might agree.[25]

Its long intellectual history should not mask the fact that the metaphor of the body politic has had different meanings and been used to make many different arguments over its long history. Like many metaphors, the body politic is often, indeed perhaps always, used as a rhetorical device.[26] Properly understood, it is used to persuade listeners or readers to adopt a particular perspective or course of action. The Roman senator's speech to the *plebs* is a classic example. As a

[24] Cary J. Nederman and Kate Langdon Forhan (eds.), *Medieval Political Theory: A Reader – The Quest for the Body Politic* (Routledge, 1993), ch. 3 'Metalogicon and Politicraticus, John of Salisbury', 27.

[25] *The Independent on Sunday*, 20 November 2005 – cited by Andreas Musolff, 'Political Metaphor and Bodies Politic' in U. Okulska and P. Cap (eds.), *Perspectives in Politics and Discourse* (John Benjamins, 2010), 24.

[26] Sarah Covington, *Wounds, Flesh and Metaphor in Seventeenth-Century England* (Palgrave Macmillan, 2009).

rhetorical device, it has been used for both good and ill purposes. Infamously, during the Third Reich, the metaphor was used for wicked purposes, where Joseph Goebbels spoke about Jewish people as parasites in the body of other people and as an infectious illness.[27]

The adoption of a metaphor such as the body politic thus ordinarily serves a rhetorical purpose that requires explanation. This book examines the role of courts in modern societies. And the body politic metaphor is used in its title to illuminate the fact that modern states, particularly those with constitutional frameworks that seek to ensure that power is held to account and that assert the rule of law and the independence of the judiciary, comprise different institutions and actors that perform different functions. These different institutions and actors are dynamically interdependent, much as parts of the body are, and their relationship is determined in part by the constitutional design, but also by questions of political and legal culture, themselves determined by many factors, notably history, politics, economics and social relations.

Courts are just one of the institutions of the modern body politic. Others include legislatures and executives, the civil service or bureaucracy, and those institutions nowadays sometimes called accountability institutions, such as electoral commissions, ombuds, central banks, media regulators and human rights commissions. Yet other institutions of the body politic are private institutions and include political parties,

[27] See the full discussion in Andreas Musolff, *Metaphor, Nation and the Holocaust: The Concept of the Body Politic* (Routledge, 2010), 2.

media organisations, the legal profession, universities, corporations and civil society actors.

The metaphor of the body politic thus captures this institutional variety and richness of modern societies, as well as the functional differentiation of these institutions and actors, all contained, at least to some extent within an interdependent dynamic organism, whose functioning is determined in part by constitutional text but often more fundamentally by constitutional practice, which in turn is a product of political and legal culture.

Law is of central importance in most contemporary bodies politic. And the consequence is, as Martin Chanock has observed, that '[n]ot only judges and legislatures speak about law, but so do people at large; religious organisations; the press; special interests such as trade unions and mining and industry; and ... so do bureaucrats.'[28] The entire body politic, therefore, engages with law, its institutions and its practices, and the manner of that engagement is crucial to how courts, constitutions and law work in any society.

The Challenge of Comparison

I turn now to consider the challenge of comparison. Although many modern societies appear from a distance to have the same or similar institutions comprising their bodies politic, and their constitutional texts may have marked similarities,

28 See Martin Chanock, *The Making of South African Legal Culture, 1902–1936: Fear, Favour and Prejudice* (Cambridge University Press, 2001), 23.

closer examination suggests that the character and practice of states vary markedly.

Recent valuable scholarship has counted the number of societies that have written constitutions, the number of societies that have courts with strong powers of judicial review and the number that have independent central banks. But these big-n studies, as social scientists call them, often miss the granularity and detail that differentiates these societies. This book seeks to assert the importance of granularity, and particularly the importance of political and legal culture in influencing how the institutions of the body politic work in different places.

Comparison is hard for two reasons. First, we come to comparison embedded in the perspectives that flow from our own experience in our own society. When we analyse other societies, our perspective often remains that of our own society, and our normative commitments within it. We should not be ashamed of our use of comparison for this purpose. One of the great benefits of comparison is to illuminate our own societies to us. By looking elsewhere, it makes us think in a different way about what is familiar and important to us. But genuine understanding of other societies requires us to work hard to see them fully, not just as some simplified pastiche. And quite often we move from the experience of our own society, and our normative commitments within it, to making general claims about other places, and asserting normative claims in general. It is that tendency of which we should be aware, and against which we should guard.

The second reason to claim that comparison is hard is that what we are comparing differs markedly. These differences mean that close attention needs to be paid not only to constitutional text but also to constitutional practice, in a thick sense, to understand how constitutions work in any specific body politic, which makes it hard actually to compare them. Accordingly, we should be cautious about asserting general principles to be applicable across different societies at different times.

The Spread of Written Constitutions and the Role of Courts

The key driver of the role of courts in the body politic in the modern era has been the spread of written constitutions. Written constitutions generally assert the sovereignty of the state, establish and regulate the institutions of government, and often entrench and protect the fundamental rights of individuals within the jurisdiction of the state. Today nearly every country in the world has a written constitution.[29] And even that small handful, which includes the United Kingdom, New Zealand and Israel, that do not have a full-length, big-C constitution, have constitutional documents that regulate the structures of government and the relationships between government and individuals.

In her fascinating account of the flourishing of written constitutions between the mid eighteenth century and the beginning of the First World War, *The Gun, the Ship and the Pen*, Linda Colley argues that the orthodox explanation which credits the American and French revolutions of the late eighteenth century, and the Haitian and Bolivarian revolutions of

[29] The text of most of the world's constitutions are usefully made available on the website of the Constitute project at www.constituteproject.org

the early nineteenth century, all of which were inspired at least in part by principles of republicanism, democracy and nation-building, for the rise of written constitutions, overlooks other key historical conditions that drove the process of constitution-making in the period.

Colley argues that 'the growth in the geographical range, frequency, intensity and demands of warfare and cross-border violence'[30] was a key driver of written constitutions. Warfare, she claims, led to the drafting of written constitutions for at least two reasons – first, sustained hybrid warfare (that is warfare both on land and at sea) put tremendous pressure on political regimes because of its cost, both human and economic, that sometimes caused the regimes engaging in warfare to fragment or collapse. The new regimes that then emerged nearly always opted for written constitutions as they reconstructed their system of government. But even those states that avoided collapse, often opted to draft and publish written constitutions, 'to rally wider support and justify expanding fiscal and manpower demands'.[31]

Colley maintains too that the age of empire, in its heyday in the last decades of the nineteenth century and first decades of the twentieth century, when eleven of the twelve most populous political jurisdictions globally were not nation states but empires, also resulted in the spread of written constitutions. During this period, imperial powers drafted constitutional documents for the territories they governed.

[30] See Linda Colley, *The Gun, the Ship and the Pen: Warfare, Constitutions and the Making of the Modern World* (Profile Books, 2021), 5.

[31] Ibid., 7.

Moving beyond the period Colley examined, into the twentieth century and the early twenty-first century, the adoption of written constitutions has continued apace. Consistent with Colley's analysis, the end of the Second World War triggered constitution-making most notably in the defeated powers of Japan and Germany but also in the many states whose boundaries were redrawn following the conflict. Shortly thereafter the end of the period of empire (which could perhaps be dated to 1922, when Ireland adopted its first Constitution) resulted in a flood of new constitutions in the newly independent postcolonial states. After the Second World War, this trend accelerated, starting with the enactment of the Indian Constitution, which came into force in 1950. Later in the century the fall of autocratic governments in Spain and Portugal resulted in new written constitutions; and then the fall of the Berlin Wall resulted in new constitutions being adopted throughout central and Eastern Europe. Since 1990, too, Latin America and Africa, particularly Eastern and Southern Africa, have seen a flood of new constitutions with most of the countries in the region adopting new constitutions since 1990.

The Conditions of Constitution-Making

Most constitutions are adopted (and amended) in what might be called, to coin Bruce Ackerman's term, 'constitutional moments',[32] when there is broad enough support in a political

[32] Ackerman's argument is developed in his important trilogy on the American Constitution: *We the People, Volume 1: Foundations* (Harvard

community to chart a new course. Many of the new constitutions adopted in the last seventy years have been adopted at times of transition or even crisis. The ending of wars, as mentioned above, is often accompanied by a flurry of constitution-making, as are the moments of transition from military dictatorships, colonial subjection, civil wars, single-party rule and political crises.

Constitutions in many settings are thus peace agreements. They are moments in which political communities seek to find a way of living together in peace. And one of the key measures of success for all constitutions, which needs little elaboration here in Belfast, is the extent to which 'the people most able to cause violence accept the basic terms [of the constitutional settlement] and are willing to process disagreements in constitutionally acceptable ways'.[33]

If constitutional moments are generally moments of transition, then they will often be uncertain times: the political community will often be fragile and the grip of the central government on the state may be precarious. Institutions of the body politic, particularly those established in the new settlement, may be brand new, as was the South African Constitutional Court in 1994, or in transition from a contentious past, in both cases charting a new course and culture. Thinking about the expanded role of courts in the modern

University Press, 1993), *We the People, Volume 2: Transformations* (Harvard University Press, 2000) and *We the People, Volume 3: The Civil Rights Revolution* (Harvard University Press, 2018).

33 See Jennifer Widner, 'Constitution Writing in Post-Conflict Settings: An Overview' (2008) 49 *William and Mary Law Review* 1513–1542, 1515.

world, therefore, requires us to remember that constitutions are generally written in turbulent times, with all the instability and uncertainty that characterise such times.

The Separation of Powers

There is a lively scholarly debate about what the separation of powers entails, and what its purpose may be.[34] Recent scholarship has begun to provide a fuller account of the separation of powers in modern constitutions. First, scholars have noted that the doctrine of the separation of powers should not be understood simply as one principle but rather as 'a close-knit set of principles that work both separately and together as touchstones of political legitimacy'.[35] These modern conceptions of the separation of powers fit well with the concept of the body politic articulated above. For these accounts of the separation of powers recognise that the different branches of government are best understood as interdependent and connected institutions performing different functions within one

[34] See, for example, C. Montesquieu, *The Spirit of the Laws*, Book 11, ch. 6 and Book 19, ch. 27; Jeremy Waldron, 'Separation of Powers and the Rule of Law' in Jeremy Waldron (ed.), *Political Political Theory* (Harvard University Press, 2016); N. W. Barber, 'The Separation of Powers' in N. W. Barber (ed.), *The Principles of Constitutionalism* (Oxford University Press, 2018); E. Barendt, 'Separation of Powers and Constitutional Government' [1995] *Public Law* 599; Aileen Kavanagh, 'The Constitutional Separation of Powers' in D. Dyzenhaus and M. Thorburn (eds.), *Philosophical Foundations of Constitutional Law* (Oxford University Press 2016); C. Möllers, *The Three Branches: A Comparative Model of the Separation of Powers* (Oxford University Press, 2013).

[35] See Waldron, n. 34, 49.

dynamic enterprise. Importantly, the close-knit set of principles that constitutes the separation of powers can produce many different constitutional frameworks, all of them arguably consistent with the separation of powers.

A final point to note is that the independence of courts and their impartiality are central to the separation of powers, in all its forms. The desirability of judicial impartiality is a defining structural element of the institution of courts, which determines their role within the constitutional framework. It is not a variable element of the separation of powers.

The Many Tasks of Courts in Modern Constitutional Settings

The emerging role of courts under the written constitutions of the last thirty years was not something that most political scientists had either predicted or proposed.[36] But under new constitutional frameworks, courts have been given an extraordinarily diverse array of responsibilities.

Firstly, as AV Dicey observed over a century ago, in federal systems where there is a division of power between a central government and regional or state governments,[37] courts generally play a central role. As Dicey puts it, '[f]ederalism … means legalism – the predominance of the judiciary in the

[36] Samuel Issacharoff, *Fragile Democracies: Contested Power in the Era of Constitutional Courts* (Cambridge University Press, 2015), 9.

[37] For a recent valuable account of how to define federalism, see Francesco Palermo and Karl Kössler, *Comparative Federalism: Constitutional Arrangements and Case Law* (Hart Publishing, 2017), 14–17.

constitution – the prevalence of a spirt of legality among the people.'[38] Many of the world's larger countries are federal in some respect, for example the United States, Australia, Nigeria, Brazil or Germany. Federations vary in how they are designed and how they work. With only a few exceptions, including Switzerland and Ethiopia, courts in federal systems play a key role in determining conflicts that arise about the allocation of powers. Federal regional conflicts are often intensely politically salient, and courts have to navigate an appropriate role in the body politic in seeking to adjudicate the disputes that arise.

Secondly, courts have in many constitutions been given the power to determine the constitutionality of legislation, which may require courts to consider whether legislation has been passed following the constitutionally prescribed procedures, and whether the legislation itself is consistent with the fundamental rights enacted in the constitution. This power, referred to by Americans as the power of judicial review, and by others as constitutional review, has been highly controversial in the Anglo-American world, but it is a power that has been conferred on courts by nearly all the constitutions enacted since the Second World War. Arguably this form of judicial power has been the most controversial for scholars, particularly in the light of the counter-majoritarian debates. I shall return to the question of the adjudication of fundamental rights and constitutional review in Chapter 3.

Thirdly, courts have often been given a role in protecting democracy. This role can take different forms.

[38] A. V. Dicey, *Introduction to the Law of the Constitution* (Macmillan, 1915), 170.

In Germany, for example, when the Nazis rose to power under the constitution of the Weimar Republic, close attention was paid in the aftermath of the war to how that could be prevented from happening again.[39] The techniques used to achieve this goal have been used in other places too and are now often referred to as 'militant democracy'. Militant democracy includes a range of tools including prohibitions on extremist, anti-democratic parties' participation in electoral processes, the exclusion of certain individuals from eligibility for standing for public office, as well as restrictions on certain forms of speech.

Fourthly, courts have sometimes been given important roles in relation to the constitution-making process itself. One of the most well-known examples, which I mentioned in my introduction, is the role conferred upon South Africa's Constitutional Court to determine whether a constitutional text adopted by the Constitutional Assembly was consistent with a set of constitutional principles that had been agreed by the key political actors in the process of transition from apartheid to democracy. The two-stage approach to constitution-making has since been followed in other countries too.

Fifthly, courts in constitutional frameworks founded on the rule of law will generally have a broad jurisdiction to determine whether the provisions of the constitution have been lawfully implemented. The consequence is that constitutional frameworks, whether intentionally or not, often confer new roles on courts.

[39] See the full discussion in Issacharoff, n. 36.

Let me take an example from the Good Friday (or Belfast) Agreement. This agreement laid the ground for the establishment of what can broadly be understood as a form of consociational government – including power-sharing in the executive, self-government and autonomy in cultural life and veto rights for minorities.[40] The agreement was given effect in the Northern Ireland Act, 1998, which as Lord Bingham later acknowledged 'is in effect a constitution',[41] establishing a single-chamber assembly and an executive branch, with powers over economic development, education, health and social services, agriculture, the environment and the civil service. Policing and the courts were originally not devolved, but were subsequently devolved in 2010.

The executive branch of government is particularly distinctive with two leaders: the first minister and the deputy first minister, offices with identical powers and functions, and individual ministers without a system of collective responsibility. The system clearly requires the two executive leaders to work together. Brendan O'Leary has suggested that 'crises over executive formation and maintenance have been the major signals that the Agreement might fail, and that remained as true in 2017 as in 1998'.[42] And one might add, that still pertains in 2022.[43]

[40] See Brendan O'Leary, *A Treatise on Northern Ireland, Volume III: Consociation and Confederation* (Oxford University Press, 2019), 178.

[41] See *Robinson v Secretary of State for Northern Ireland and Others* [2002] UKHL 32, para. 11.

[42] O'Leary, n. 40, 184.

[43] The political impasse in Northern Ireland relating to the appointment of the first minister and deputy first minister that arose after the May 2022

In a constitutional system founded on the rule of law, it is not surprising that the Northern Ireland Act, 1998 has been the subject of judicial consideration on many occasions. One of the earliest of those occasions was the case of *Robinson v Secretary of State for Northern Ireland and Others*.[44] In that case, Peter Robinson, a Democratic Unionist member of parliament (MP), challenged the appointments of the first minister and deputy first minister by the assembly, on the basis that their appointments had taken place two days outside of the then six-week period stipulated in the Northern Ireland Act[45] within which the appointments should take place. A majority of the House of Lords adopted a purposive and contextual approach to the interpretation of the Northern Ireland Act, and they decided that the appointments were nevertheless valid. Lord Bingham emphasised that 'ordinary constitutional practice in Britain' often leaves 'matters of potentially great importance' to the judgment either of political leaders or even to the Crown. He noted that 'where constitutional arrangements retain scope for the exercise of political judgment they permit a flexible response to differing and unpredictable events in a way which the application of strict rules would preclude'.[46] Lord Hoffmann

elections, when the Democratic Unionist Party (DUP) refused to agree to the appointment of the first minister and deputy first minister, was only resolved in February 2024, when the DUP ended its boycott of the power-sharing arrangements and Michelle O'Neill became the first nationalist politician to serve as the first minister.

44 *Robinson*, n. 41.

45 Section 16 of the Northern Ireland Act, 1998. The period has since been extended to twenty-four weeks.

46 See *Robinson*, n. 41, para. 12.

in his concurrence reasoned that the interpretation of the Act contended for by the appellant was 'contrary to the Agreement's fundamental purpose, namely to create the most favourable constitutional environment for cross-community government. This must have been foreseen as requiring the flexibility which could allow scope for political judgment in dealing with the deadlocks and crises that were bound to occur.'[47] *Robinson* is a surprising case, given the majority's willingness to accept that the election of the executive was lawful despite it not falling within the explicitly legislated time frame.[48]

Robinson is not the only challenging case to have arisen following an impasse concerning the appointment of the executive under the Northern Ireland Act. Another challenge was the question of whether civil servants would have the power to grant large planning applications in the absence of a functioning executive. Ordinary constitutional doctrine provides that it is ministers who make planning decisions, and who are accountable for them. That was the approach adopted in *Buick*,[49] in which the Court of Appeal in Northern Ireland held that civil servants did not have the power to exercise powers conferred upon ministers unless legislation had also clearly conferred the power upon civil servants. The Westminster Parliament sought to fill this void in government in Northern Ireland by enacting legislation to enable departments to exercise ministerial

[47] Ibid., para. 30.

[48] See the discussion in Andras Gal, 'Beyond "Unwinding": Constitutional Review Strategies in Consociations' (2020) 26 *Nations and Nationalism* 594–610.

[49] *Re Buick (judicial review)*, [2018] NICA 26.

functions where it is in the public interest to do so for a specified period when the Northern Ireland executive has not been formed.[50] Time does not permit an analysis of that legislation, but that it was enacted indicates the complexities that have arisen with the body politic in the United Kingdom as a result of the ongoing political contestation in Northern Ireland around the power-sharing arrangements provided for in the Good Friday Agreement.

It is not only under written constitutions that courts are called upon to determine constitutional questions. Brexit, which amended some of the key elements of the United Kingdom's famously unwritten constitution, has given rise to a wealth of interesting and contentious jurisprudence (not surprising, perhaps, given how politically contentious Brexit has been). The two *Miller* cases are both examples of this,[51] as is the pending case before the Supreme Court, *Allister and others for Judicial Review (Northern Ireland)* concerning the Northern Ireland Protocol.[52] And it is not over yet: clause 7 of the newly published Retained European Union Law (Revocation and Reform) Bill 2022[53] confers a

[50] The first enactment, following the decision in *Buick*, was the Northern Ireland (Executive Formation and Exercise of Functions) Act, 2018.

[51] See *R (on the application of Miller and Another) v Secretary of State for Exiting the European Union* [2017] UKSC 5 and *R (Miller) v The Prime Minister; Cherry v Advocate General for Scotland* [2018] UKSC 41.

[52] See the discussion in Anurag Deb, 'The Union in Court: *Allister and Others' Application for Judicial Review* [2021] NIQB 64' (2022) 73(1) *Northern Ireland Legal Quarterly* 138–161.

[53] Tabled in parliament on 22 September 2022. See clause 7(3) which substitutes the test provided in section 6(5) of the European Union

novel and broad discretion on the courts in determining whether to depart from retained European Union law. The Brexit process provides an excellent example of how modern constitutional frameworks, sometimes intentionally, and at other times not, expand the work of courts.

Why Are Courts Given These Expanded Roles? And What Determines How They Perform Them?

Modern constitutions thus confer a range of politically sensitive and contested roles upon courts. For these constitutions to work, as Samuel Issacharoff has put it, they 'must rise from the desks of [their] authors and take form in the governing institutions of a society'.[54] Two questions about the expanded role of courts arise: Why are courts given these expanded roles? And what determines whether they will perform the roles conferred upon them by written constitutions?

The first question has been the most investigated in comparative constitutional research, which has demonstrated that the expanded role of courts, particularly where explicitly provided for in the constitutional text, has been driven by powerful political actors who have seen expanding the role of courts as protecting their own interests. In an early influential study, for example, Tom Ginsburg concluded that political elites confer the power of constitutional review upon courts as

Withdrawal Act, 2018. It could potentially include Retained EU Law (Revocation and Reform) Act 2023.

54 See Issacharoff, n. 36, 14.

a form of insurance against the risk that they will lose political office in future.[55]

The second question, when do courts exercise their constitutional powers effectively, has been the subject of less investigation, perhaps because it is methodologically more challenging.[56] In some cases, it is clear, the powers conferred upon courts may not be exercised at all. The phenomenon of constitutions not constraining political actors has long been recognised. James Madison spoke about constitutions as 'parchment barriers',[57] and modern scholars have investigated the phenomenon of 'sham constitutions'.[58]

But in most cases, constitutions are not entirely sham.[59] For the political actors that brought the written constitution into force generally have some level of commitment to it.

[55] Tom Ginsburg, *Judicial Review in New Democracies: Constitutional Choices in Asian Cases* (Cambridge University Press, 2003). See also, Ran Hirschl, *Towards Juristocracy: The Origins and Consequences of the New Constitutionalism* (Harvard University Press, 2004); Tom Ginsburg and Mila Versteeg, 'Why Do Countries Adopt Constitutional Review?' (2013) 30 *Journal of Law, Economics and Organisation* 587–622; Tom Ginsburg and Ros Dixon, 'The Forms and Limits of Constitutions as Political Insurance' (2017) 15 *International Journal of Constitutional Law* 988–1012.

[56] See David Law, 'Constitutions' in Peter Cane and Herbert Kritzer (eds.), *Oxford Handbook of Empirical Legal Research* (Oxford University Press, 2010), but see the recent collection byTom Ginsburg and Aziz Huq (eds.), *From Parchment to Practice, Implementing New Constitutions* (Cambridge, 2020).

[57] See James Madison, *The Federalist, No. 48*, 1 February 1788.

[58] See David Law and Mila Versteeg, 'Sham Constitutions' (2013) 101 *California Law Review* 862–952.

[59] See Ginsburg and Huq, n. 56, 7–8.

But how courts perform their functions is dependent on a range of factors that have not been fully investigated by social scientists. One reason for this relates to how social scientists theorise judicial decision-making. Political scientists tend to view judicial decisions as forms of political decision, while economists tend to view them as decisions designed to achieve optimal outcomes.[60] For the most part, neither considers whether judges and other legal actors really make decisions in the same way as political or economic actors.[61]

In a recent important study, Theunis Roux has argued that in studying the phenomenon of modern written constitutions (his study is specifically focussed on the practice of strong form judicial or constitutional review), we should start by recognising that the relationship between law and politics is conceived differently in different constitutional cultures. In the United States, for example, 'widespread cynicism prevails about whether the justices of the Supreme Court are capable of privileging their good-faith interpretation of the law over their ideological loyalties in high-profile constitutional cases like those involving abortion, or the right to bear arms, or same-sex marriage'.[62] In Germany, on the other hand, Roux notes, 'the idea that there exist quasi-scientific

60 See Gillian Hadfield, Jens Meierhenrich and Barry Weingast, 'A Positive Theory of the Rule of Law' in Jens Meierhenrich and Martin Loughlin (eds.), *The Cambridge Companion to the Rule of Law* (Cambridge University Press, 2021), 237–258, 245. See also Theunis Roux, *The Politico-Legal Dynamics of Judicial Review: A Comparative Analysis* (Cambridge University Press, 2018).

61 Hadfield, Meierhenrich and Weingast, n. 60, 245.

62 See Roux, n. 60, 65.

legal reasoning techniques, like proportionality, through which members of the Federal Constitutional Court might be able to accord appropriate weight to competing political values is less controversial'.[63]

Some recent scholarship has begun to look more closely at questions of political, legal and institutional culture in considering what makes it possible for courts to perform their role.[64] As Paul Kahn has rightly noted, 'establishing a constitution is not merely a matter of writing a text, but of creating a culture that mediates between legal text and political power. Because power is never wholly controlled by law, the transition from revolution to constitution is never really finished. It is not an event that happens but a sort of existential condition carried forward in a set of practices and beliefs. Those can be more or less fragile.'[65]

Culture is of course a troublesome category particularly for those social scientists who wish to measure and compare.[66]

[63] Ibid.

[64] See, for example, Michaela Hailbronner, *Traditions and Transformations: The Rise of German Constitutionalism* (Oxford University Press, 2016); Lisa Hilbink, *Judges beyond Politics in Democracy and Dictatorship: Lessons from Chile* (Cambridge University Press, 2007); Roux, n. 60; Maria Popova, *Politicised Justice in Emerging Democracies: A Study of Courts in Russia and Ukraine* (Cambridge University Press, 2012); Kathryn Hendley, *Everyday Law in Russia* (Cornell University Press, 2017).

[65] Paul W. Kahn, 'Constitutional Culture: Opening a Space between Law and Power' (2019) 189 *Telos* 15–33, 17.

[66] See David Nelken, 'Comparative Legal Research and Legal Culture: Facts, Approaches and Values' (2016) 12 *Annual Review of Law and Society* 45–62. See also Tom Ginsburg and James Melton, 'Does the

Its precise boundaries are uncertain, although it seems clear that it contains ideological elements, such as attitudes, beliefs and values, and behavioural elements, such as practices. But the fact that constitutional culture may be difficult to define, measure and compare is not sufficient reason to ignore it if it helps us illuminate the differences between societies and to understand how bodies politic work.

The question of legal culture brings me back to where I began: that first week in which the Constitutional Court of South Africa began to consider how it should perform the constitutional role that had been conferred upon it. In the discussions that week, the Court began to articulate an account of its institutional culture and values.

In developing the institutional values of the Court that week, key aspects of existing legal culture were retained or rejected. The new values were signalled not only in the rules of the court, but also in its symbols. The Court's logo, the tree under which people sheltered, drew both on the concept of indigenous justice in southern Africa, where disputes are heard and decided by traditional leaders in the open before the community, and on the explicit new role to be performed by the court for protecting fundamental rights. In rejecting the colonial era honorifics of His Lordship and Her Ladyship, the court signalled a rejection of the hierarchical colonial legacy and an embrace of a more democratic conception of the role of judges. The moment of transition from apartheid to democracy was an opportune moment for

Constitutional Amendment Rule Matter at All?' (2015) 13 *International Journal of Constitutional Law* 686–713.

the court to establish its values and persona. Not every court in every constitutional structure has such a propitious beginning. However, there remains deep contestation within the body politic about South Africa's values and direction. Contestation is, after all, the project of democracy, whose future, we should never forget, is not certain.

2

Courts and the Executive Branch

Introduction

In Chapter 1, I made four key points:

- The role that courts play in modern bodies politic has expanded significantly as a result of the practice of writing constitutions, either as big-C constitutions as in South Africa, or in legislation of constitutional significance as in Northern Ireland and Brexit.
- The expanded role of courts has often been driven by political actors in circumstances of fragility and uncertainty.
- It is helpful to recognise that courts are institutions within the broad body politic and that the body politic comprises not only the branches and institutions of the state but also actors, often characterised as private institutions, such as political parties, the media, civil society and the legal profession. Whether courts can play the roles conferred upon them effectively will thus depend not only on the legal and institutional culture of the court but also upon the institutions, relationships and culture of the broader body politic.
- Responding to the expanded role of courts with a simple normative claim that it is democratically inappropriate for courts to perform these roles may reflect an idealised account of how politics works in many places, indeed perhaps everywhere, coupled with a failure to grasp the

> fragile and precarious character of the body politic at the time of constitution-writing in many modern societies. In a time of global democratic recession increasingly characterised by executive aggrandisement, it is perhaps also unwise.

In this chapter, I turn to the relationship between courts and the executive branch of government. In many ways, this relationship is the 'make or break' relationshiop for courts. The executive branch is ordinarily the most powerful branch of government, and when courts act to hold the executive to account, they are often at their most vulnerable. But the charged relationship between courts and the executive arises not only from the political tension that is generated by holding a powerful executive to account but also from the different structural and functional characteristics of the executive and the judiciary.

I will commence by outlining key structural and functional characteristics of the judiciary and the executive. Then I will turn to three situations that kindle tensions between the executive and courts: first, the relationship between courts and the executive in states that are authoritarian or illiberal, or becoming so. Here the tension between the executive and the courts ordinarily arises because the executive is seeking to prevent the courts functioning as accountability mechanisms, although this is not an iron rule. Sometimes authoritarian states have tolerated courts acting independently to hold government to account.

The second situation that gives rise to tensions between the executive and courts is times of crisis or emergency, whether war, political crisis, a health emergency, such as the COVID-19 pandemic or a climate-induced emergency.

Here the tension arises because the executive needs to act fast, and the processes of accountability lag behind and often become politically contentious.

A third setting in which the tension between the executive and courts is exacerbated is where individuals in the high executive are widely perceived to be, or are in fact, using their offices for personal gain in a corrupt manner. Under these circumstances, where legal processes are initiated in courts to hold members of the high executive to account, political actors often turn on the courts and question their impartiality, competence and fairness. The institutional reputation of courts within the body politic is then in peril.

Understanding the Functional Characteristics of Courts

In thinking about the relationship between the courts and the executive, it will be important to start with a brief account of the character and functioning of each. In orthodox constitutional theory, courts are independent of the other two arms of government, and they adjudicate disputes brought before them by members of the public. They determine the disputes according to law after a fair process in which the parties to the case before them have been afforded an opportunity to make arguments as to how the case should be decided. Key characteristics of courts include the following:

1. Unlike the legislature and the executive, courts are generally reactive. Ordinarily they are empowered to act only when disputes are brought before them. And the facts and law in

those disputes are generally framed by the parties. One of the consequences of courts being reactive is that they have a limited capacity to choose what issues they would like to hear. Some apex courts, like the US Supreme Court, have control over their docket – that is, they are not required to hear a case unless they decide to hear it. This permits a court to pick and choose between those cases that are brought to it but not generally to initiate cases themselves. Not all apex courts have control over their dockets, and some apex courts are compelled to hear appeals where there is an appeal as of right or where leave to appeal has been granted by another court. Unusually, the Indian Supreme Court has developed a jurisdiction referred to as its Public Interest Litigation jurisdiction, which permits the court of its own accord to identify issues that require its attention. The consequence of the reactive character of courts is that once they have decided a matter, and in particular, where they have adopted a particular interpretation of the law or applied the law in a particular way to a set of facts, they cannot adjust or alter their decisions unless the matter is returned to them, a matter over which they have little or no control. And even when it is returned to them the principle of legal certainty and the doctrine of precedent mean that courts will generally be slow to reverse an earlier decision. In this regard, courts differ markedly from legislatures and executives who can act proactively in developing the law and change laws as they think fit.

2. Courts must act fairly and impartially in deciding cases. In most legal systems, judges are obliged to comply with codes of conduct that require them to act consistently with the impartiality and independence that their judicial office

requires. Moreover, judges must make their decisions with fidelity to law, in the light of the arguments they have heard. Lon Fuller memorably described the process of adjudication as being defined by the form of participation it affords the litigants: that is the right to present proof (or evidence) and reasoned argument in favour of their case in order to persuade the judge to find in their favour.[1] Fuller argued that the consequence of this definition of adjudication was that 'it gives formal and institutional expression to the influence of reasoned argument in human affairs' and 'assumes a burden of rationality not borne by other forms of social ordering'[2] such as negotiation or voting.

3. Once we accept Fuller's definition of adjudication, it follows that judges need to give reasons for the decisions they make. Cases rarely reach senior appellate courts if their outcome is beyond doubt, and the reasons given in judgments aim to persuade the audience that the outcome in the case is correct. Even if the audience may not be persuaded of the correctness of the outcome, the judgment still needs to persuade the audience that the court has acted impartially and competently in determining the dispute. There are different styles of written judgments in different legal systems, and judgments need to accord with the traditions of their own system to be persuasive.[3] The

[1] Lon L. Fuller, 'The Forms and Limits of Adjudication' (1978) 92 *Harvard Law Review* 364.

[2] Ibid., 366.

[3] For a recent fascinating empirical investigation of the different modes of judicial reasoning in nineteen different jurisdictions, see Andras Jakab,

audience for a decision will vary depending on the case.[4] In a collegial court, the first audience is often the judge's colleagues. Where the tradition is to seek one judgment of the court to promote legal clarity, then the first object of a draft judgment is to persuade a judge's colleagues to concur. Once the judgment is delivered, the audience will always include the parties to the case and their lawyers, and will often extend, particularly in legal systems where precedent serves as a source of law, to other lawyers, judges and legal scholars. Where a case is of public importance, the audience for judgments will also include many others in the body politic including politicians, journalists and members of civil society, and again the judgments will seek to persuade those audiences that the decision is correct, and at the least that the judgment is competent and fair-minded. And increasingly in the modern world, the audience will include judges and lawyers in other legal systems.

4. Courts mostly work slowly: a case involves the exchange of pleadings by the parties, at times the leading of oral evidence, argument by the parties, and then the process of decision-making by the court. A first instance decision is often followed by an appeal, a process that takes time. And sometimes, a second appeal follows. Courts can act expeditiously in some circumstances, but what is fast for a court remains relatively slow for other actors.

Arthur Dyevre and Giulio Itzcovich (eds.), *Comparative Constitutional Reasoning* (Cambridge University Press, 2017).

[4] See Lawrence Baum, *Judges and Their Audiences: A Perspective on Judicial Behavior* (Princeton University Press, 2008).

5. Judges are generally not democratically elected, although there are some notable exceptions including in the United States, Switzerland and Bolivia. Instead, judges are ordinarily appointed by the executive or legislature, or some combination of them. To preserve their independence, judges are also generally protected from removal from office save in exceptional circumstances, and they are protected against reduction in their salaries and benefits. Nevertheless, despite the protections provided in constitutional design, judges are vulnerable to pressures, particularly from the executive arm of government. It is not uncommon to find the executive branch issuing veiled or even direct threats against the judiciary that relate to their tenure and/or their conditions of service.
6. Courts are not able to implement the orders they make. Sentences of imprisonment are carried out by the executive, and orders to pay damages made against members of the public are ordinarily implemented at the instance of the successful party. Alexander Hamilton famously described courts as 'the least dangerous branch' of government because they controlled no armies and had no independent spending power.[5] Given the expansion of judicial power that I have been describing, and the current contestation over the US Supreme Court, Hamilton's description may be less current today than then, but it does

[5] Alexander Hamilton, *The Federalist No. 78*, 28 May 1788. Alexander Bickel titled his seminal work on the US Supreme Court *The Least Dangerous Branch: The Supreme Court at the Bar of Politics* (Bobbs-Merrill, 1962).

capture the inter-institutional powers of courts quite accurately. Courts are not powerful unless their orders are implemented by the other branches of government.

These six characteristics of courts – that they are reactive, rather than proactive; that they must decide cases fairly, impartially and with fidelity to law; that they must give reasons for their decisions; that they function slowly rather than quickly; that they are not democratically accountable; and that they have no institutional control over the implementation of their judgments – distinguish them from the legislature and executive. These institutional characteristics inevitably structure what courts can do and what they cannot, so their function in the body politic is in large part driven by their functional and structural characteristics.

The traditional model of adjudication is triadic in form, as identified many years ago by Martin Shapiro,[6] based on the prototype of two parties who are in dispute seeking a third party to assist them resolve the dispute. When courts resolve disputes in this model of adjudication, they look backward to determine facts that have occurred, identify the relevant legal rules and then apply those rules to the facts. But there is another model of adjudication, the public law model, which has developed as a result of the expanded role of courts in modern constitutional settings.[7] The public law model of litigation is different. It relates to disputes about constitutional

[6] Martin Shapiro, *Courts: A Comparative and Political Analysis* (University of Chicago Press,1981), ch. 1.

[7] See Abram Chayes, 'The Role of the Judge in Public Law Litigation' (1976) 89 *Harvard Law Review* 1281–1316.

or public law rights in which the litigation is often forward-looking to vindicate the rights of many people, some of whom will be parties to the litigation and others who are not parties, and where the remedies are not fully determined by the formulation of the litigants' claim. This public law model of adjudication was first described in the United States, but it is now to be found in many constitutional settings, particularly in those where courts are empowered to protect fundamental rights. Perhaps the leading courts globally in this model of litigation are those in India and Colombia.

Despite the differences between the dispute resolution and public law models of adjudication, the six characteristics of courts do not ordinarily vary. Courts remain reactive (with the notable exception of the model of public interest litigation in India in which courts initiate litigation themselves)[8] and are obliged to act fairly, impartially and with fidelity to law and to give reasons for their decisions, which means that they tend to act more slowly, with judges appointed rather than elected, and reliant upon others to implement their decisions.

Understanding the Functional Characteristics of the Executive Branch

The executive branch is quite different. As Paul Craig and Adam Tomkins have noted: 'Executive power . . . is the political power that all those who embark on a career in politics

[8] See Anuj Bhuwania, *Courting the People: Public Interest Litigation in Post-Emergency India* (Cambridge University Press, 2017).

dream of wielding. It is the power to set policy, to take action to implement the law . . . the preserve of the executive is to *do*.'[9] In one of the early discussions of the executive branch of government, Alexander Hamilton famously argued that '[e]-nergy in the executive is a leading character in the definition of good government. It is essential to the protection of the community against foreign attacks: it is not less essential to the steady administration of the laws. . . A feeble executive implies a feeble execution of government.'[10]

Hamilton here points to what arguably are the two key functions of the modern executive branch. The first is to protect the state and its inhabitants. This duty to protect concerns external threats, such as times of warfare against foreign states, but it extends as well to internal threats, such as terrorism, civil war or insurrection, environmental harms, natural disasters, such as earthquakes, and major health crises. In contrast to the other two branches of government, executives can and must be able to act quickly and decisively.

The second duty is to govern. In the modern era, this involves not only making policy and implementing the legislation adopted by the legislature but also legislating administratively across large swathes of public life. In the modern urbanised world, the public is dependent upon the state for the provision of many basic services, notably water and electricity, and also for shelter, education, transport links and, in

[9] See Paul Craig and Adam Tomkins, *The Executive and Public Law: Power and Accountability in Comparative Perspective* (Oxford University Press, 2005), 1.

[10] Alexander Hamilton, *The Federalist No. 70*, 15 March 1788.

many countries, basic healthcare. Although the legislature will legislate to determine what services must be provided, it is the executive that must actually ensure delivery.

An important distinction that exists in all forms of executive government is between what I shall call the high or core executive, on the one hand, and administrators, on the other. The high executive consists of the president or prime minister and the political heads of departments that carry out the work of government. The high executive is the primary bearer of the duty to protect and thus ordinarily leads in the building of relationships with other states, and often has oversight over the military and other security services. In addition, the high executive often initiates government policy. The second key role of the executive, for which the high executive takes political responsibility, but which is carried out by the administration, is the responsibility for implementing the legislation enacted by parliament. Increasingly, in the modern world, the executive makes rules; delegated or secondary legislation promulgated by the executive branch far exceeds parliamentary legislation in most contemporary bodies politic. In democracies, the high executive is generally politically accountable either directly to the voters, or indirectly, in the case of parliamentary systems, to representatives elected by the voters.

The administrators are those members of the executive, who are not democratically elected, but employed to implement legislation. In modern states, there are many thousands of administrators (often called bureaucrats or civil servants) employed by the government to provide services and to carry out legislative policy. It is perhaps the executive branch of government that has grown most considerably since the eighteenth century when modern accounts of the separation of powers were first developed. In his recent book, Martin Loughlin recalls that during his presidency, George Washington had more slaves working at Mount Vernon than the number of people employed in the executive presidency. Today, the US federal government employs more than nine million people, and its annual budget amounts to more than $4 trillion, that is 20 per cent of gross national product.[11]

As I have said, in contrast to the other two branches of government, the high executive can and must be able to act quickly and decisively. Yet the executive must also act in accordance with law. There is a tension between these two requirements, and the fundamental challenge for liberal democracies is to find ways of ensuring that the high executive is accountable for its conduct, without imperilling its ability to function effectively.

There are different ways in which the executive can be held to account. First, it can be held to account by the legislature, and in many constitutional frameworks this is a core function of the legislature. A second mechanism for accountability is democratic election, which can be by members of the legislature, in parliamentary democracies where the head of the executive, often called the prime minister, is elected. Election by the legislature often follows an internal election within the governing political party (where the head of the executive is appointed by the majority party in

[11] Martin Loughlin, *Against Constitutionalism* (Harvard University Press, 2022), 62.

the legislature). Alternatively, the head of the executive, often called the president, may be directly elected by members of the public. Elections, whether within political parties or general elections, ordinarily occur only infrequently but they nevertheless cast a long shadow. That shadow is extended by the work of the media in publicising the conduct of the executive. Thirdly, there are specialised independent accountability agencies in many countries, such as ombuds, that oversee the work of the executive. And finally, there are courts. Which of these mechanisms of accountability are dominant in a particular body politic will depend on a variety of factors including the nature of the constitution, particularly whether it is a written constitution where the powers of the executive are set out as legal rules or whether it is an unwritten constitution where the executive's powers are better understood as constrained by convention and political practice rather than law, and by the political and legal culture.

But all these mechanisms are hampered by four characteristics of executive conduct that render it resistant to being held to account: the core importance of its responsibility to protect the body politic and its inhabitants is the first, because in acknowledging this responsibility accountability mechanisms often, and often rightly, consider that they should defer to the decisions of the executive in this area. Second, the range and variety of the activities of the executive; third, the speed with which the executive branch can and at times must act; and fourth, the relative inscrutability of executive decision-making and action all make the task of accountability difficult. Often by the time accountability mechanisms attempt to bring executive conduct into focus, the conduct has happened, and the process of oversight becomes unavoidably backward-looking. Moreover, finding out what has actually happened is not straightforward.

Just over ten years ago, Eric Posner and Adrian Vermeule wrote a controversial book about the executive in the United States, arguing that not only did the executive act often in breach of the law but also that the law was unable to constrain such conduct effectively, and, more surprisingly, that it did not matter as other forms of non-legal control, particularly politics and public opinion, prevent the executive acting in a tyrannical fashion.[12] Their account was disputed, with scholars arguing that the evidence suggested that American presidents do act in a manner, at least most of the time, consistent with their being constrained by law.[13] There was general agreement, however, that mechanisms of accountability for president were imperfect, although public opinion and politics are important.

I am not as sanguine as Posner and Vermeule that we need not worry about the frailty of the accountability mechanisms to ensure that the US president, or for that matter the executive branch in any other polity, acts lawfully and in the public interest. As worrying is the fact that the Donald Trump presidency was not a global outlier. The last twenty years have seen a pattern of decay in democracies across the world. Whether one looks at the annual reports produced by

[12] See Eric Posner and Adrian Vermeule, *The Executive Unbound: After the Madisonian Republic* (Oxford University Press, 2011).

[13] See Richard Pildes, 'Law and the President' (2012) 125 *Harvard Law Review* 1381–1424, 1386–1387.

Freedom House, *Freedom in the World*, the *Economist Intelligence Unit* Democracy Index or V-Dem's Democracy Reports, the message is clear. Democracy is in decline. And one of the key characteristics of the decline has been the expansion of executive power. The pattern varies across different societies, but it seems widespread.[14] The global concentration of executive power has led one constitutional scholar to suggest that 'constitutional dictatorship' should replace 'democratic deficits' and the 'American obsession' with the 'counter-majoritarian difficulty' as the central concern of constitutional theory.[15]

We need therefore to think carefully about modes of accountability of the executive, while acknowledging the need, as Hamilton put it, to avoid inappropriately sapping the energy of the executive. In her recent study of the executive branch of government in the United States and the United Kingdom, Margit Cohn argues that the tension between prompt and effective executive action, and the need for the executive to act lawfully and to be held to account, is resolved by a range of legal rules that are, as she calls them, fuzzy because they lack sharp criteria or clear modes of enforcement.[16] She argues that

[14] See Mark A. Graber, 'What's in Crisis? The Postwar Constitutional Paradigm, Transformative Constitutionalism and the Fate of Constitutional Democracy' in Mark A. Graber, Sanford Levinson and Mark Tushnet (eds.), *Constitutional Democracy in Crisis?* (Oxford University Press, 2018), 682.

[15] Ibid.

[16] See Margit Cohn, *A Theory of the Executive Branch: Tension and Legality* (Oxford University Press, 2021).

what she calls fuzzy law both undermines the rule of law and damages citizen participation and deliberation.

Perhaps somewhat surprisingly, Margit Cohn's primary solution to the problem of fuzzy law is to call on courts to adopt enhanced modes of review of such rules so as to promote executive accountability and to offer members of society a different forum for voicing concerns and contributing to public deliberation. Interestingly, Cohn is less concerned about ensuring that the legislature should avoid enacting fuzzy rules in the first place. Although Cohn's argument that a tension will often arise between an effective executive branch and an accountable one, I am not persuaded that there is a 'one size fits all' solution to that tension across different bodies politic, which would suggest that courts are the primary institution to enhance the accountability of the executive. The mechanisms to hold the executive to account need to be adapted to the particular characteristics of each body politic. Courts will have a role to play, but what that role will be will vary across different settings.

A Troublesome Trio: Illiberalism, Emergencies and Corruption

I turn now to consider three particularly challenging contexts for courts when seeking to hold the executive branch to account. These contexts are firstly, illiberal or authoritarian states; secondly, crises or states of emergency; and thirdly, endemic corruption. All these contexts present special, though different, challenges for courts.

Illiberalism and Authoritarianism

There is a complex relationship between courts and authoritarian governments. One might assume that courts will never, or at best rarely, act independently in authoritarian societies to hold the executive branch to account. Yet the role of courts in authoritarian societies has been the subject of increasing investigation by comparative constitutional scholars, and the picture is more complex than one might assume.

In his early influential study of courts, Martin Shapiro noted that in public law cases, appeal processes often provide central government with information about what lower-level administrative officials are doing, and so enhance the ability of central government to control the administration.[17] Tamir Moustafa's groundbreaking study of courts in Egypt under President Anwar Sadat demonstrated that despite being an authoritarian leader, President Sadat enhanced the capacity and jurisdiction of administrative law courts during his tenure, which had been restricted under President Nasser in 1959.[18] Sadat did this to provide an avenue for redress to citizens and to expose corruption in the state bureaucracy at the time that the government's policy was to move towards a mixed economy and to attract foreign direct investment. Moustafa also notes that the overall record of the courts during President Sadat's period in office was

[17] Shapiro, n. 6, 49–50.

[18] See Tamir Moustafa, 'Law and Resistance in Authoritarian States: The Judicialization of Politics in Egypt' in Tamir Moustafa and Tom Ginsburg (eds.), *Rule by Law: The Politics of Courts in Authoritarian Regimes* (Cambridge University Press, 2008), 145.

patchy. In particular, he records that the Egyptian Supreme Constitutional Court upheld the constitutionality of a rule that insulated the emergency state security court system from the ordinary legal system with the consequence that cases brought against political opponents of the government were brought in the state security courts where the rules of due process were sharply attenuated.

Relying on this and several other examples, Moustafa and Ginsburg argue that relatively stable authoritarian governments may be more likely to permit courts to function in an independent fashion. A relatively stable authoritarian government may be able to 'experiment' with judicial independence in order to promote economic growth, enhance its global reputation and generate tax revenues. Authoritarian governments that are more precarious, or are in the process of being established, may be less able to do so.[19]

The converse may also be true. When the high executive branch sets out on an authoritarian or illiberal path, it is often likely to take steps to limit the power of courts that may otherwise seek to hold it to account. We have seen such processes under way in both Poland and Hungary over the last decade.

Wojciech Sadurski's account of how the Law and Justice party in Poland, having won narrow majorities in both the presidential and parliamentary elections in 2015, sought to emulate the changes that Viktor Orban had introduced in Hungary after he was re-elected for a second term in 2010, makes compelling, if depressing, reading. Sadurski notes that

[19] Ibid, 11.

the Law and Justice programme of action included attacks on civil society organisations, new legislation to constrain the media, disempowering and capturing the Constitutional Court, removing judges by lowering the retirement age and appointing others perceived to be more favourable to law and justice, restructuring independent accountability institutions such as the National Council of the Judiciary and the electoral commission, and identifying the EU as a foreign, hostile association that interferes illegitimately in the affairs of member states.[20]

These steps taken by Law and Justice in undermining courts and judicial independence, restricting media freedom, restricting the functioning of civil society organisations, including universities, the capture of independent guarantor organisations like electoral commissions and judicial appointment bodies and spurning international law and its norms constitute what might be described as the contemporary authoritarian playbook. In the current global environment, which has seen the rise of populist parties and leaders on every continent, this playbook has been widely followed in different bodies politic in different parts of the world.

Populism presents a particular challenge here. Cas Mudde has defined populism as an ideology 'that considers society to be separated into two homogenous and antagonistic groups, "the pure people" versus "the corrupt elite", and which argues that politics should be an expression of the

[20] Wojciech Sadurski, *Poland's Constitutional Breakdown* (Oxford University Press, 2019), 4.

volonté général (general will) of the people'.[21] This is a narrow definition based on a particular (unfortunately common) form of populism.

Populist politicians tend to emphasise the importance of popular sovereignty and they prefer forms of direct democracy, such as referendums, over institutions of accountability such as courts, and also over institutions of representative democracy, such as legislatures. Populist leaders emphasise their direct link with the people, dismissing those who disagree with them 'as the corrupt elite' or 'outsiders'. Populist leaders tend to disparage not only interventions by courts or other independent agencies that seek to hold them to account, on the grounds that they are attempting to frustrate the democratic will of the majority, but they also challenge democratically elected legislative bodies that seek to hold them to account.

One of the great difficulties for liberal democracies is to distinguish between those constitutional and legislative reforms that are legitimate and those that are not.

Often these are the very questions that arise in courts when piecemeal illiberal reform is challenged, and these questions are not easy for courts to answer. And when courts do consider that the executive has acted in a manner inconsistent with the law or constitutional framework, then, as we have seen in many parts of the world, such as Poland and Hungary, the risk is that the executive will pursue an agenda that will undermine the ability of the court to act impartially, and/or

[21] Cas Mudde, 'The Populist Zeitgeist' (2004) 39 *Government and Opposition* 543.

its powers to hold the executive to account. It is for this reason that the appointment and removal of judges, the diminution of their benefits, whether salaries or pensions, changes in the composition of courts, or curtailment of their jurisdiction, are often suspect.

Emergencies and Crises

A second set of circumstances in which the tensions between the executive branch and courts are amplified are times of crisis or emergency. If a primary function of the executive branch is to protect the state and its inhabitants, then when emergencies arise, the executive must act. It is emergencies, as many scholars have observed, that present the greatest challenge to liberal democracies. This is because the protections that liberal democracy provides may need to be attenuated in times of emergency to enable the government, and particularly the executive branch, to respond quickly and effectively to protect the body politic.[22]

Emergencies come in many shapes and sizes, and they are increasingly global. In the last two decades, we have experienced the emergency responses to international terrorism in the wake of 9/11, 7/7 and other attacks and to COVID-19, and we are increasingly encountering the emergency responses required to address environmental hazards resulting from global climate change.

[22] See, for example, John Ferejohn and Pasquale Pasquino, 'The Law of the Exception: A Typology of Emergency Powers' (2004) 2 *International Journal of Constitutional Law* 210–239.

The challenge of how to govern during an emergency was perhaps first addressed in the Roman Republic, when a dictator was appointed in times of emergency to address urgent perils. As Machiavelli put it:

> A dictator was made for a time and not in perpetuity, and only to remove the cause for which he was created; and his authority extended only in being able to decide by himself the ways of meeting that urgent peril, to do things without consultation, and to punish anyone without appeal; but he could do nothing to diminish the State, such as would have been the taking away of authority from the Senate or the people, or to destroy the ancient institutions of the City and the making of new ones.[23]

There are some who argue that in an emergency, ordinary law does not apply.[24] The emergency constitutes what Carl Schmitt called a state of exception.[25] And many scholars have argued that in real emergencies, the constitution and protection of liberty must give way.[26] However, not all

[23] Niccolò Macchiavelli, *Discourses on Livy*, ch. 34 (1517), cited in Ferejohn and Pasquino, n. 22, 211.

[24] See, for example, Richard Posner, *Not a Suicide Pact: The Constitution in a Time of National Emergency* (Oxford University Press, 2006) and William H. Rehnquist, *All the Laws but One: Civil Liberties in Wartime* (Vintage Books, 2000).

[25] See Carl Schmitt, *Political Theology: Four Chapters on the Concept of Sovereignty* (University of Chicago Press, 2005, first published 1922), 10.

[26] See, for example, Clinton L. Rossiter, *Constitutional Dictatorship: Crisis Government in the Modern Democracies* (Princeton University Press, 1948) and Giorgio Agamben, *State of Exception* (University of Chicago Press, 2005).

scholars take this view. Others have argued that it is possible to manage emergencies without surrendering core constitutional protections.[27]

Given that emergency situations are frequent, varied in source and enduring, it is not surprising that it has become increasingly common for modern constitutional frameworks to include provisions that regulate emergencies and today ninety per cent of modern constitutions contain provisions to do so.[28] Emergency provisions generally address five questions: in what circumstances may an emergency be declared? Who declares the emergency? Who exercises the emergency powers? Who decides that the emergency has ended? And what accountability mechanisms exist to ensure that emergency powers are exercised lawfully?[29] Eighty per cent of constitutions with emergency provisions give the head of state the power to declare a state of emergency, but then nearly forty per cent require at least one chamber of the legislature to approve that declaration, thus seeking to establish a check on the executive.[30] And over a third now impose time limits

27 See, for example, David Dyzenhaus, *The Constitution of Law: Legality in a Time of Emergency* (Cambridge University Press, 2006) and Nomi Claire Lazar, *States of Emergency in Liberal Democracies* (Cambridge University Press, 2009).

28 See Christian Bjornskov and Stefan Voigt, 'The Architecture of Emergency Constitutions' (2018) 16 *International Journal of Constitutional Law* 101–127.

29 See Ferejohn and Pasquino, n. 22, 230, who identify the last four of these questions and Bjornskov and Voigt, n. 28, who identify these five and a sixth: what additional competences does a state of emergency confer on government.

30 See Bjornskov and Voigt, n. 28, 108–109.

on states of emergency that may be extended only with legislative approval.[31]

Emergency provisions in constitutions are invoked not infrequently. Bjornskov and Voigt found that 137 countries had declared states of emergency at least once between 1985 and 2014.[32]

The global COVID-19 pandemic has presented us with a remarkable set of data on just how emergencies are handled across the globe, which researchers are now beginning to examine.[33] The global practice was remarkably varied: some countries, such as France, Chile, Namibia and Jordan, used their constitutional emergency powers, but others, including Germany, the Netherlands, Japan and South Africa, used existing statutory frameworks for disasters or crises, and yet others, including the United Kingdom, enacted new legislation.[34]

The role for courts in the management of emergencies largely concerns the question of how to ensure that emergency powers are exercised lawfully. There are institutional and structural reasons why courts are often not able to perform this role successfully. In emergencies, the structural, functional and institutional differences between courts and the executive branch are at their most acute. Courts generally accept that it is a core function of the executive to protect a

[31] Ibid. [32] Ibid., 101.

[33] See, for example, Avi Weiss, 'Binding the Bound: State Executive Emergency Powers and Democratic Legitimacy in the Pandemic' (2021) 121 *Columbia Law Review* 1853–1894.

[34] See Tom Ginsburg and Mila Versteeg, 'States of Emergencies: Part 1' *Harvard Law Review Blog*, 17 April 2020.

body politic in emergency situations and that the executive must act quickly and effectively to do so. Courts thus approach challenges to executive conduct during an emergency conscious of the core institutional responsibility of the executive and the need to avoid unduly impairing the responsive capacity of the executive branch. Courts' ability to assess the facts is also often hampered by the fact that it is the executive branch that has those facts, and they are not always accessible to courts. Even where they are, courts are reluctant to second guess an assessment of peril made by the executive branch.

It is thus perhaps not surprising that the record of courts on protecting the fundamental rights of foreign citizens in wartime, or in restricting the powers of the executive during emergencies is as David Dyzenhaus puts it, 'at worst dismal, [and] at best ambiguous'.[35] Striking examples include the decision of the House of Lords in *Liversidge v Anderson* (which concerned a damages claim brought by a person who had been detained under emergency powers),[36] the US Supreme Court decision in *Korematsu v US* (upholding the evacuation of Japanese Americans from the West Coast of the United States during the Second World War to enable their internment)[37] and for me, at least, closer to home, the decision of the then South African Appellate Division in *Omar v Minister of Law and Order* (upholding emergency regulations

[35] See Dyzenhaus, n. 27, 17. See also Bruce Ackerman, 'The Emergency Constitution', 113 (2004) *Yale Law Journal* 1029 and Cass Sunstein, 'Minimalism at War' [2004] *The Supreme Court Review* 47–109.

[36] [1942] AC 206. [37] 323 US 214 (1944).

that deprived those who had been indefinitely detained without trial from access to counsel).[38] Dyzenhaus argues, I think rightly, that upholding the rule of law, especially in times of emergency, needs a range of institutions in the body politic, including legislatures, courts and other institutions, to foster it. Dyzenhaus uses a different metaphor, calling these various institutions 'rule of law furniture', and says that without them judges will not be effective bulwarks against breaches of the rule of law.[39] Despite the difference in metaphor, the underlying premise is the same: courts are not going to be strong bulwarks against executive abuse of power in emergencies, unless there are other organs in the body politic that support their role.

In determining how to enable courts to play a robust role in ensuring accountability and the rule of law during states of emergency, it is important to start by recognising that their institutional and structural characteristics hamper their capacity to do so, and that they cannot act effectively in isolation. How a constitutional system should seek to bolster the rule of law in times of emergencies will depend on its own constitutional design, as well as on its history and political and legal culture. I am optimistic that we will learn from the experience of the pandemic in how to manage emergencies, but like Dyzenhaus, I think the starting point is ensuring that courts are not on their own in seeking to ensure the rule of law during emergencies: legislatures and other organs of the body politic need to serve as mechanisms of accountability too.

[38] 1987 (3) SA 859 (A). [39] See Dyzenhaus, n. 27, 230.

Corruption

Corruption by members of the executive branch of government, both the high executive and administrators, remains a persistent problem in the world. Definitions of corruption vary, but Transparency International's definition 'the abuse of an entrusted power for private gain' captures the core proposition that people who have been entrusted with a responsibility misuse it to further their own private interests.[40] Transparency International's global Corruption Perceptions Index shows that levels of corruption worldwide remain high, though apparently not increasing. Two-thirds of the 180 countries measured have serious corruption problems, and 131 countries have made no significant progress against corruption in the last decade, often despite apparently seeking to reduce corruption.[41] The 2021 Transparency International Corruption Perceptions Index report also demonstrated that there is a correlation between high levels of corruption, as measured on the Index, and infringements of civil and political rights. As Transparency International points out, this relationship works in both directions: fewer civil liberties make it harder to hold corrupt

[40] See www.transparency.org (last accessed on 24 September 2022). See also discussion of the definition in Susan Rose-Ackerman and Bonnie J. Palifka, *Corruption and Government: Causes, Consequences and Reform*, 2nd ed. (Cambridge University Press, 2016).

[41] See Transparency International Corruption Perceptions Index 2021, available at www.transparency.org/en/cpi/2021 (last accessed on 23 September 2022).

governments to account, and corrupt governments often restrict civil liberties.[42]

One would ordinarily expect in a democracy that elections would serve as a core accountability mechanism against corruption, and that political leaders who are or who are perceived to be corrupt would be punished at the polls. Although this does often happen, it does not always happen, and often to a more limited extent than you would expect.[43]

The question then arises of how courts fare as accountability mechanisms in relation to corruption on the part of the executive. Corruption by the executive branch comes before courts in several ways. Firstly, and most obviously, if members of the high executive are prosecuted for offences related to corruption, such as bribery and extortion, those trials take place in court. Secondly, there are a range of other disputes relating to corruption that may end in court. For example, administrative decisions, such as procurement, that are alleged to have been tainted by corruption may well be challenged in court. In addition, the conduct of other accountability mechanisms such as ombuds or prosecutors may be challenged in court either by those alleged to have acted corruptly or by those who argue that the mechanisms have failed to act.

[42] Ibid.

[43] See, for example, Michael Johnston, 'How Do I Vote the Scoundrels Out? Why Voters Might Not Punish Corrupt Politicians at the Polls' (2013) 60 *Crime, Law and Social Change* 503–514; Andreas Bagenholm, 'Throwing the Rascals Out? The Electoral Effects of Corruption Allegations and Corruption Sscandals in Europe' (2013) 60 *Crime, Law and Social Change* 595–609.

First let us discuss prosecutions. The prosecution of former or sitting heads of state was exceedingly rare before 1990,[44] but that has changed in the last thirty years. Between 1990 and 2008, sixty-seven current or former heads of state were prosecuted for criminal misconduct while in office. About half of these prosecutions were for offences relating to corruption. One of the reasons for the increased number of prosecutions may have been shifting global attitudes towards corruption. Those changing attitudes were reflected in the adoption, in 2005, of the UN Convention against Corruption, which by 2021 had been ratified by 189 countries. The convention requires states to adopt legislation to ensure that specified examples of corrupt conduct constitute criminal offences including bribery of public officials, embezzlement and misappropriation of property by public officials for their own benefit.[45] The convention also requires states to establish independent anti-corruption bodies, in accordance with the fundamental principles of its legal system.[46]

However, research has shown that prosecuting the high executive presents particular challenges. Firstly, corruption cases are hard legally: finding evidence to establish the facts of corruption is difficult because illegal payments and bribes are skilfully concealed, and even where a payment can be shown, establishing that the defendant made or received the payment with the requisite corrupt intent is also often difficult. Secondly, corruption trials of political leaders are

[44] See Ellen Lutz and Caitlin Reiger, *Prosecuting Heads of State* (Cambridge University Press, 2009).

[45] See chapter 3 of the convention.

[46] See article 6 of the convention.

ordinarily conducted 'in the full glare of the media spotlight' and 'whereas most judges are unaccustomed to conducting judicial business in such an environment, the political leaders on trial are in their element in a politicised arena and usually are highly skilled at playing to a public audience'.[47] Ensuring a fair trial in these difficult circumstances requires highly skilled judges.

Yet the game may often be worth the candle. Though not always. As Lutz and Reiger observe,

> the symbolic value of head of state trials depends on the quality of the process and the 'demonstration effect' it is seen to have for strengthening the rule of law. If conducted transparently and in a way that inspires the general population's confidence in the process, they can contribute to ending pervasive traditions of impunity, and demonstrate that no one is above the law, no matter how far up the political or military chain of command. The risks of politicisation, however, are never far away.[48]

The risk is that political actors being prosecuted for corruption will politicise the project by suggesting that both prosecutors, who bring cases against political leaders, and courts, who may convict them, are acting for political reasons. Politicising anti-corruption criminal processes in this way is perilous for courts. In Italy, for example, voters differ on whether courts should be trusted and supported as impartial actors based on their political affiliations, with a higher proportion of centre-left voters trusting courts than centre-right

[47] See Lutz and Reiger, n. 44, 283. [48] Ibid., 285.

voters.[49] In highly political polarised societies, particularly where a populist leader is charged, this risk is real.

A different problem arises when prosecutors pursuing corrupt executive actors, and courts in adjudicating the cases that arise, adopt innovative procedures or rules. In the famous Lava Jato (Car Wash) scandal in Brazil in which a prosecuting magistrate investigated an enormous corruption scandal involving political leaders of the Workers Party (former President Luiz Inacio 'Lula' da Silva was prosecuted and convicted), a controversy arose as to whether the innovations adopted were consistent with the rule of law and international human rights.[50] A key example is that the courts held that President Lula's receipt of gifts from private companies constituted corruption, without any proof that the companies received any benefit (what might be called a quid pro quo) from President Lula.[51] This was a novel interpretation of the relevant provision of the Criminal Code at the time and was contested by legal scholars. There were other innovations in legal doctrine as well, which were also contentious. In the end, the Brazilian Supreme Court overturned the

[49] See Salvatore Sberna and Alberto Vannucci, 'It's the Politics, Stupid! The Politicisation of Anti-corruption in Italy' (2013) 60 *Crime Law and Society* 565–594, 590.

[50] See Mariana Mota Prado and Marta R. de Assis Machado, 'Using Criminal Law to Fight Corruption: The Potentials, Risks and Limitations of Operation Car Wash' (2021) 69 *American Journal of Comparative Law* 834–879. See also Mark Tushnet, 'Institutions Supporting Constitutional Democracy: Some Thoughts about Anti-corruption' (2019) *Singapore Journal of Legal Studies* 440–455.

[51] Mota Prado and de Assis Machado, n. 50, 847.

conviction of former President Lula in April 2021 and then held that the investigating magistrate who had led the investigation was biased. What the Lava Jato case illustrates is that prosecutions of members of the high executive will be closely scrutinised, and where innovations are introduced may be highly contested.

The second category of cases concerning corruption are those cases that are not criminal prosecutions but in one way or another relate to corruption. South Africa has seen a series of these arising from corruption scandals over the last several decades. I will select just one: the South African Constitution provides for a range of institutions to support constitutional democracy including an electoral commission, a public protector (or ombud), an auditor-general and a human rights commission.[52] These are all independent institutions with special processes for appointment and removal.

In 2011 and 2012, the public protector received a series of complaints from members of the public, including a member of parliament, requesting that she investigate security upgrades being made to then President Zuma's private residence in Nkandla, KwaZulu-Natal on the basis that lavish improvements were being made, which were not related to security. Following her investigation, the public protector produced a report,[53] concluding that many of the

[52] See chapter 9 of the South African Constitution, 1996.

[53] Public Protector, *Secure in Comfort: Report on an Investigation into Allegations of Impropriety and Unethical Conduct Relating to the Installation and Implementation of Security Measures by the Department of Public Works at and in Respect of the Private Residence of President Jacob Zuma at Nkandla in the KwaZulu-Natal Province*, March 2014.

improvements could not be classified as security measures, including a visitors' centre, a cattle kraal, a chicken run, an amphitheatre and a swimming pool, and that accordingly there had been a misuse of state funds. As remedial action, the president was to refund a reasonable percentage of the improvements, the amount to be determined with the assistance of the National Treasury, to reprimand the ministers involved and to report to the National Assembly on what he had done.[54] Following the report of the public protector, the president requested the minister of police to investigate and determine what he should do in response to the report, and the National Assembly also commissioned a report from the minister. The minister of police reported that the improvements that the public protector had found not to be security-related improvements were in fact security-related and concluded that the president did not have to take any remedial steps. The National Assembly and the president accepted the minister's report. Their decision to do so was challenged as unconstitutional. The Constitutional Court held that the president's failure to comply with the remedial action stipulated in the public protector's report and the resolution of the National Assembly absolving the president from complying with the remedial action in the report were unconstitutional. It ordered that the National Treasury should determine a reasonable percentage of the costs of the non-security improvements and require the president to repay it.

[54] See *Economic Freedom Fighters v Speaker of the National Assembly and Others* [2016] ZACC 11, para. 10.

There were several novel aspects of this decision: firstly, it had not been clear until the decision whether remedial action recommended by the public protector was binding or not. This judgment answered that question affirmatively. Secondly, it was also not clear whether the National Assembly was bound to hold the president accountable in the event of adverse findings by the public protector. Here again the court held that it was so bound, unless it challenged the findings of the protector in court.[55] 'Neither the President nor the National Assembly,' the court held 'was entitled to respond to the binding remedial action taken by the public protector as if it is of no force or effect'.[56] The third novel aspect of the court's decision was its order setting aside a resolution made by parliament, which had been made in the proper form, but which the court held to be unconstitutional.[57]

For those raised in a constitutional framework based on parliamentary sovereignty and article 9 of the 1689 Bill of Rights, it is this last innovation which may raise eyebrows.[58] This decision is one of a series in which the South African courts have required the president and parliament to act consistently with

[55] Ibid., para. 97. [56] Ibid., para. 99. [57] Ibid., paras. 98–99 and 105.

[58] 'That the freedom of speech and debates or the proceedings of Parliament ought not to be impeached or questioned in any court or place out of Parliament', UK Bill of Rights, 1689, article 9. See the full discussions in Firoz Cachalia, 'Precautionary Constitutionalism, Representative Democracy and Political Corruption' (2019) 9 *Constitutional Court Review* 45–81; Aziz Huq, 'A Tactical Separation of Powers Doctrine' (2019) 9 *Constitutional Court Review* 19–44; Stephen Gardbaum, 'Pushing the Boundaries; Judicial Review of Legislative Procedures in South Africa' (2019) 9 *Constitutional Court Review* 1–18.

their constitutional mandate. A few months after the Nkandla case, the public protector issued another report on the issue of 'state capture' – that is the question whether members of the high executive in South Africa, including President Zuma, had an improper and corrupt relationship with a prominent business family, the Guptas.[59] The public protector recommended that a commission of inquiry be appointed to investigate the question. President Zuma unsuccessfully challenged the public protector's report in court,[60] and, in accordance with the court's order, the chief justice then appointed deputy chief justice Raymond Zondo to chair a commission of inquiry into the allegations of state capture. The commission was appointed in early 2018 and issued its final report during 2022.

It is important to acknowledge that in the South African example, a range of institutions within the body politic worked together to ensure accountability. In addition to the courts and the public protector, the opposition political parties who brought the litigation and raised debates in parliament, journalists and the media who led the investigations into many of the corrupt practices, and civil society organisations all worked towards this. It may

[59] See *State of Capture: Report of an investigation into alleged improper and unethical conduct by the President and other state functionaries relating to alleged improper relationships and involvement of the Gupta family in the removal and appointment of Ministers and Directors off State-Owned Enterprises regulating in improper and possibly corrupt award of state contracts and benefits to the Gupta's family businesses* (Public Protector, South Africa, Report 6 of 2016/2017) dated 14 October 2016. Available at www.gov.za/sites/default/files/gcis_document/201611/stateofcapturereport14october2016_1.pdf

[60] See *President of the Republic of South Africa v Office of the Public Protector and Others* [2017] ZAGPPHC 747.

well be that this strong alliance tempered the public contestation around the role played by the public protector and the South African courts but their roles have been contested, at least by former President Zuma and his allies. There is also no doubt that the consequences of this series of litigation, notably through the hearings and reports of the State Capture Commission, has resulted in the exposure of widespread corrupt practices especially in state-owned enterprises including Transnet, South African Airways and the electricity utility, Eskom. What the long-term consequences will be, remains uncertain.

Conclusion

In conclusion, what can be said about the relationship between courts and the executive branch in the body politic? There is no single answer to this question. Like many relationships, this is a complex and difficult relationship in every constitutional setting. Understanding the structural and functional characteristics of both parties in the relationship helps us to understand something of the character of the relationship, but this will differ across different settings. Modern societies need effective and energetic executive branches, but holding them to account and ensuring they act in the public interest is a challenging project. Courts are one mechanism of accountability, together with the legislature, regular elections and the media, but how well any of these mechanisms of accountability work will depend on a range of political, historical, social and economic factors, both within the borders of the relevant body politic and beyond them.

3

Courts and Human Rights

Oxford, 16 November 2022

Introduction

The theme of this book is courts in the body politic, and the earlier chapters have made four core arguments.

- The role that courts play in modern bodies politic has expanded significantly as a result of the practice of writing constitutions, either as big-C constitutions as in India, Ireland or South Africa, or in legislation of constitutional significance.
- The expanded role of courts has often been driven by political actors in circumstances of fragility and uncertainty.
- It is helpful to recognise that courts are institutions within the broad body politic of their own society. The body politic is an old political metaphor that has been used to sustain many arguments, not all of them benevolent, over the centuries. The use of such a metaphor requires both explanation and justification. In this book, it is used to illuminate the fact that in most modern states there are different institutions and actors that affect how the state is governed. These institutions are dynamically interdependent, just as parts of the body are, and their relationship is determined not only by constitutional design but also by questions of political and legal culture, determined by many factors, history, politics, economics and social relations. The body

politic thus comprises not only the branches and institutions of the state but also what are often characterised as private institutions, such as political parties, the media, civil society and the legal profession. The metaphor thus captures both the institutional variety and richness of modern societies, and also the functional differentiation of these institutions and their dynamic interdependence. The role that courts play in a body politic depends not only on the constitutional text, and the institutional and legal culture of courts, but also upon the institutions, relationships and culture of the broader body politic.

- The book seeks to destabilise the simple normative claim that it is democratically inappropriate for courts to perform these expanded roles, arguing that such claims may reflect an idealised account of how politics works in many places, indeed perhaps everywhere, coupled with a failure to grasp the fragile and precarious character of the body politic at the time of constitution-writing in many modern societies. In a time of global democratic recession increasingly characterised by executive aggrandisement, such claims are also perhaps unwise.

This chapter turns to one of the most contested aspects of the expanded role of courts: human rights.

On 10 December 1948, the United Nations adopted the Universal Declaration of Human Rights (UDHR). The Preamble to the Declaration begins:

> Whereas recognition of the inherent dignity and of the equal and inalienable rights of all members of the human family is the foundation of freedom, justice and peace in

> the world and whereas disregard and contempt for human rights have resulted in barbarous acts which have outraged the conscience of mankind and the advent of a world in which human beings shall enjoy freedom of speech and belief and freedom from fear and want has been proclaimed as the highest aspiration of the common people...

In the thirty brief clauses that followed, the UDHR proclaimed civil and political liberties,[1] as well as economic, social and cultural rights, including a right to social security,[2] a right to education[3] and a right to a standard of living adequate for health and wellbeing.[4] Forty-eight countries voted in favour of the adoption of the UDHR, and eight abstained, including the Soviet Union, Saudi Arabia and South Africa, where the National Party government had been elected only months before on the basis of its manifesto policy to introduce apartheid.

The adoption of the UDHR was an extraordinary achievement.[5] That in the aftermath of terrible conflict, and at a time of deep political disagreement, it was possible to produce a document expressing a global commitment to treating human beings equally and with respect was astonishing and momentous.

[1] See UDHR, articles 3–21. [2] Ibid., article 22. [3] Ibid., article 26.

[4] Ibid., article 25.

[5] Zachary Elkins and Tom Ginsburg, 'Imagining a World without the Universal Declaration of Human Rights' 74 (2022) *World Politics* 327–366, 329.

It may be, as Mark Mazower has argued, that the UDHR was made possible because it did not impose legal obligations upon states.[6] Yet the UDHR nevertheless constituted, as another scholar, Andrew Moravcsik, claimed, 'a fundamental challenge not just to the Westphalian ideal of state sovereignty that underlies realist international relations theory and classical international law but also – though less-frequently noted – to liberal ideals of direct democratic legitimacy and self-determination. The post-war emergence of these arrangements has rightly been characterized as the most "radical development in the whole history of international law"'.[7]

It was nearly twenty years before the rights declared in the UDHR became legally binding on those states that ratified the International Covenant on Civil and Political Rights (ICCPR) and the International Covenant on Economic, Social and Cultural Rights (ICESCR), which were adopted in the mid-1960s. Sir Egerton Richardson, Jamaica's first representative to the United Nations, who chaired the UN Human Rights Commission in the mid-1960s, was a major driver of the adoption of the treaties, overcoming the resistance to their adoption from both the west and the Soviet Union and its satellite states.[8]

[6] Mark Mazower, 'The Strange Triumph of Human Rights, 1933–1950' (2004) 47 *The Historical Journal* 379–398.

[7] See Andrew Moravcsik, 'The Origins of Human Rights Regimes: Democratic Delegation in Postwar Europe' (2000) 54 *International Organisation* 217–272, 218.

[8] See Steven Jensen, *The Making of International Human Rights: The 1960s, Decolonization and the Reconstruction of Global Values* (Cambridge University Press, 2016).

Together, these two covenants are known as the International Bill of Rights, and their adoption was another extraordinary achievement led largely by nations from the global south, newly liberated from their colonial rulers. Today the ICCPR has 171 state parties, and only twenty countries have not ratified it at all; and the ICESCR has 168 state parties. In addition to the international covenants, there are also regional human rights treaties: the three most important being the European Convention on Human Rights (ECHR) adopted in 1950, which now has forty-seven member states, the American Convention on Human Rights adopted in 1969 with twenty-four member states and the African Charter on Human and Peoples' Rights adopted in 1986, which has fifty-three signatories.

In a recent article, Zachary Elkins and Tom Ginsburg have shown that the UDHR has had a significant (and continuing) impact on the drafting of domestic constitutions in the decades following its adoption. They conclude that the UDHR has been influential in the drafting of domestic bills of rights, noting a distinct pattern whereby rights in the UDHR were increasingly reproduced in domestic constitutions in the years following its adoption.[9] A significant number of constitutions expressly reference the UDHR. For example, the Preamble to Egypt's 2014 Constitution states that 'we are drafting a Constitution that paves the way to the future for

[9] See Elkins and Ginsburg, n. 5, 351. See also Zachary Elkins, Tom Ginsburg and Beth Simmons, 'Getting to Rights: Treaty Ratification, Constitutional Convergence and Human Rights Practice' (2013) 54 *Harvard International Law Journal* 61–96.

us, and which is in line with the UDHR, which we took part in the drafting of and approved'.[10] And the constitutions of both Moldova and Romania stipulate that the fundamental rights entrenched in them will be interpreted in accordance with the UDHR.[11] Elkins and Ginsburg plausibly speculate, on the basis of their study, that if the UDHR had not been adopted, national constitutions would likely contain fewer rights, and in particular, a smaller core of consensual rights, and that 'the societies governed by these rights are today very different places to live because of these rights'.[12]

This book discusses two key questions relating to the way courts function in bodies politic across the globe. The first question – an empirical one, primarily addressed in the Chapter 1 – is what is the constitutional role of courts in modern constitutional settings? The answer, I suggested, is that written constitutions have conferred an expanding and varying array of functions on courts over the last 200 years, but particularly since the end of the Second World War. Yet the specific role courts play is only partly determined by constitutional text. There are a range of other factors as well, including political and constitutional culture.

The second question (addressed in this chapter in relation to the executive branch of government, and to be addressed this evening in relation to fundamental rights) is whether it is possible to make general, normative claims about the roles that courts should play in modern constitutional settings. The answer to this question in relation to the executive branch of government was a cautious yes, although I asserted that the

[10] Elkins and Ginsburg, n. 5, 354. [11] Ibid., 355. [12] Ibid., 358.

precise role courts play to hold the executive to account will need to be adapted to the constitutional framework of a given society. This chapter will conclude with a perhaps less cautious yes, in relation to the adjudication of rights, although it will echo the caveat in the earlier chapters, that the role courts can and should play in a given body politic needs to be developed within the particular constitutional framework, including the political and legal culture, of that society.

This chapter will explore three questions: firstly, what role domestic courts play in the adjudication and protection of rights in different domestic constitutional settings? Secondly, what role should courts play in the adjudication of rights? And thirdly, what conclusions can we draw from these investigations for current debates in the United Kingdom concerning a possible repeal of the Human Rights Act (HRA) 1998 and withdrawal from the ECHR?

Domestic Protection of Human Rights by Courts

International human rights law recognises that constitution-making is a sovereign process that enables the people of a particular territory to determine the structures of their government. Thus, international human rights law does not dictate to countries how to structure their constitutional frameworks. It simply requires countries to meet their international human rights law obligations through whatever constitutional structure they establish.[13]

[13] See article 1 of both the ICCPR and ICESCR.

Today most countries have written constitutions. Yet there is a wide array of constitutional systems and practice across the different bodies politic in the world. That array means that the institutional structure through which states meet their obligations under international human rights treaties varies considerably. That variability is not inconsistent with international human rights law. It is relevant, however, when seeking to answer the question of what role courts play in the protection of rights. I identify seven elements of constitutional frameworks that shape how courts adjudicate rights. There is substantial variability in each of the elements, which affects precisely how courts protect rights in a particular setting.

The first element of constitutional design that may vary with respect to rights protection is whether there is a written constitution, and whether it contains a bill of rights. At the time that the UDHR was adopted, only a handful of countries had adopted constitutionally entrenched bills of rights, but that has changed in the last three quarters of a century, and now more than 80 per cent of countries in the world have written constitutions that contain a justiciable bill of rights.[14]

Yet there are still some countries that do not have a constitutional bill of rights. Many of the countries that do not

[14] See Elkins and Ginsburg, n. 5, and also Tom Ginsburg and Mila Versteeg, 'Why Do Countries Adopt Constitutional Review?' (2013) 30 *Journal of Law, Economics and Organisation* 587–622, 587, who calculated that in 1951 only 38 per cent of constitutional systems had constitutional review (which does not necessarily imply a bill of rights, but often does), whereas by 2011, 83 per cent of countries had a form of judicial review.

have constitutional bills of rights are constitutional systems based on parliamentary sovereignty and in some, but not all of them, a legislative bill of rights has been enacted to protect rights – New Zealand is a good example. Its 1990 bill of rights is contained in an Act of Parliament and is based on the ICCPR. It empowers courts to determine whether delegated legislation and the conduct of administrators are consistent with the bill of rights; but it does not empower courts to strike down as invalid legislation that is inconsistent with the bill.

Similar, but not identical in design, is the United Kingdom's HRA, an Act of the UK Parliament, which renders the ECHR domestically enforceable. The UK HRA deftly accommodates both the doctrine of parliamentary sovereignty and the principled commitment to the protection of fundamental rights, by expressly authorising courts to declare legislation to be incompatible with the rights in the ECHR and by also providing that such declarations have no force unless parliament acts upon them.[15] Although the New Zealand Bill of Rights Act did not explicitly confer the power upon courts to make declarations of inconsistency, the New Zealand Supreme Court has recently held that the legislation impliedly conferred that power upon the courts.[16] The New Zealand Parliament has now enacted amending legislation to the New Zealand Bill of Rights Act to provide that the executive should draw any declaration of inconsistency to the attention of the legislature and provide a report to

[15] See HRA, section 4.

[16] See *Attorney-General v Taylor* [2018] NZSC 104.

the legislature advising of the government's response to the declaration.[17]

Second, constitutions (and domestic legislation) vary as to which rights they protect. Some rights are nearly always protected, such as a general right to equality, entrenched in 97.8 per cent of all written constitutions in 2013, and the right to freedom of expression, protected in 94.6 per cent of constitutions,[18] but other rights are not common across constitutions at all. The right to bear arms, for example, famously entrenched in the US Second Amendment, has never been widely accepted across the world, with only 9.5 per cent of constitutions containing it in 1945, a proportion that dropped to 1.1 per cent of constitutions in 2013.[19] Overall, the rights in the UDHR, and particularly civil and political rights, are the rights most commonly found in contemporary written constitutions, but there are a significant number of constitutions that protect economic, social and cultural rights as well. The UDHR has also not served as a complete barrier to novel rights. The right to a healthy environment, which is not protected in the UDHR (although just last year the Human Rights Council passed a resolution recognising that access to a healthy and sustainable environment is a human right), was protected in only 9.5 per cent of constitutions in 1945 but is now found in 70 per cent of constitutions.

Third, the language in which rights are formulated also differs considerably. Take for example the right to

[17] See section 7A of the New Zealand Bill of Rights (Declarations of Inconsistency) Amendment Act 2022.

[18] See Elkins and Ginsburg, n. 5, 359, table A1.

[19] Ibid., 362, table A2.

equality mentioned above: article 7 of the UDHR states that 'All are equal before the law and are entitled without discrimination to equal protection of the law. All are entitled to equal protection against discrimination in violation of this Declaration and against any incitement to such discrimination.' Article 14 of the ECHR (which was drafted shortly after the UDHR) is different. It states that 'the enjoyment of the rights and freedoms set forth in the Convention shall be secured without discrimination on any ground such as race, sex, colour, language, religion, political or other opinion, national or social origin, association with a national minority, property, birth or other status'. The list of prohibited grounds of discrimination has become more common since – sometimes it is a closed list (so new grounds of discrimination may not be added), and sometimes it is open, as in the case of section 15 of the Canadian Charter of Rights and Freedoms, which was adopted in 1982, and came into force in 1985. It provides that 'Every individual is equal before and under the law and has the right to the equal protection and equal benefit of the law without discrimination and in particular without discrimination based on race, national or ethnic origin, colour, religion, sex, age or mental or physical disability.' It goes on to state that the clause 'does not preclude any law, program or activity that has its object the amelioration of conditions of disadvantaged individuals or groups including those that are disadvantaged because of race, national or ethnic origin, colour, religion, sex, age or mental or physical disability'. So, in addition to an open-ended list of grounds of discrimination, the Canadian Charter clarifies that programmes aimed at ameliorating disadvantage will not constitute a breach of the equality clause. These different formulations of the right to equal protection of the law often influence how they are interpreted.

Fourth, different constitutional frameworks regulate differently the interaction with international human rights law. There is of course the well-known monist/dualist divide: in some countries, international law and obligations properly assumed under international law by that country, automatically form part of domestic law; in others, international law, and particularly treaty obligations, only become part of domestic law when adopted formally by a legislative process. The divide between monist and dualist systems is much less sharp than often assumed, but there remains significant variability in the legal impact of international human rights obligations in domestic law. One of the ways in which the distinction is blurred arises from interpretive clauses in bills of rights or constitutions. For example, although South Africa is considered to be a largely dualist jurisdiction, the South African Constitution obliges courts when interpreting rights in the bill of rights to 'consider international law'.[20] The South African courts have read 'international law' in this provision in a broad manner to include not only binding but also non-binding international law.[21] Another important aspect of international law for domestic rights adjudication is whether a country is a member of a regional human rights treaty system, such as the European Convention of Human Rights, the Inter-American Convention on Human Rights and the

[20] See section 39(1)(b) of the South African Constitution.

[21] *S v Makwanyane and Another* [1995] ZACC 3, para. 35.

African Charter on Human and Peoples' Rights. These three regional systems all have courts that hear cases brought by individuals alleging the infringement of their rights by one of the states that is a party to the relevant treaty. The relationship between the regional human rights court and domestic courts that enforce rights differs across the three systems, and across the countries within the regional systems. I shall consider later the current debates in the United Kingdom around the HRA, which gives domestic legal effect to the provisions of the ECHR in the United Kingdom and has a carefully crafted provision regulating the relationship between the European Court of Human Rights and the UK courts.

Fifth, and importantly, Bills of Rights, whether constitutional or legislative, provide differently for the limitation of rights. Under the ECHR, for example, some rights are referred to as absolute rights because the Convention does not contemplate their limitation. Absolute rights under the ECHR include the right to be free from torture (article 3) and the right not to be held in slavery or servitude (article 4). Other rights under the ECHR expressly contemplate limitation, and they are often referred to as qualified rights. An example is article 8, which protects the right to respect for private and family life, home and correspondence. It may be limited in accordance with the law when 'it is necessary in a democratic society in the interests of national security, public safety or the economic well-being of the country, for the prevention of disorder or crime, for the protection of health or morals, or for the protection of the rights and freedoms of others'. Under the ECHR qualified rights each have their own qualification.

However, other constitutional systems do not acknowledge a distinction between absolute and qualified rights. Under the Canadian Charter, for example, all rights and freedoms are subject 'to such reasonable limits prescribed by law as can be demonstrably justified in a free and democratic society'.[22] Similarly, section 5 of the New Zealand Bill of Rights Act provides that the rights and freedoms in the bill 'may be subject only to such reasonable limits prescribed by law as can be demonstrably justified in a free and democratic society'.[23] And section 36 of the South African Constitution also contains a general limitation clause of this sort.

Courts often interpret limitation clauses as requiring the application of a proportionality test. Although there are different models of the proportionality test in different jurisdictions, a common version requires a court to ask whether a limitation seeks to achieve a lawful purpose, is rationally connected to that purpose, is the least invasive means to achieve that purpose and the extent of the limitation of the right is proportionate to the purpose that is sought to be achieved. The use of proportionality as a mechanism for weighing whether an infringement of a right is justified is jurisprudentially controversial. What is clear is that adopting a proportionality test affects the conception of rights – what we understand a right to be. Once it is accepted that there are circumstances in which rights limitations may be justifiable, then rights are not absolute. Rights do not, to use Ronald Dworkin's metaphor, automatically trump other interests.

[22] See section 1 of the Canadian Charter of Rights and Freedoms.

[23] See section 5 of the New Zealand Bill of Rights Act, 1990.

Sixth, another variable pattern in bills of rights is whether the bill of rights is amendable and if so, how easily. The question arises in relation to constitutional bills of rights as legislative bills of rights are normally amendable by ordinary legislation. Amendability is important as it is one of the ways in which the legislature can respond to a court decision concerning rights. If, for example, the court interprets a right in a particular way, and the legislature is dissatisfied with that interpretation, and the bill of rights is amendable, then the legislature may amend the law to reflect its preference.[24] In some constitutions, Namibia, for example, the bill of rights may not be amended at all. It is an 'eternity' provision. In other constitutions, the bill of rights may be amendable but only with special majorities, often heightened majorities, and special procedures.[25] The Canadian Charter of Rights and Freedoms famously contains an innovative override clause, providing that both the Canadian parliament and provincial legislatures may enact legislation that is inconsistent with the Charter, although such legislation is subject to a five-year sunset clause.[26] The override clause is not an amendment process, but, like an amendment process, it provides a pressure valve when there is disagreement between courts and legislatures on the interpretation of rights.

Seventh, when courts may determine challenges to legislation based on rights varies across constitutional

[24] See Rosalind Dixon and David Landau, 'Tiered Constitutional Design' (2018) 86 *George Washington Law Review* 438–512, 455–461.

[25] Ibid.

[26] See section 33 of the Canadian Charter of Rights and Freedoms.

settings. In most constitutional settings, legislation may only be challenged once it has come into force, by someone who has been adversely affected, but this is not a universal rule. Until 2010 in France, the Conseil Constitutionnel could only review legislation for constitutional compliance once it had been adopted by the legislature but before it was signed into law by the executive. Now, however, the Conseil may entertain requests from litigants to review whether the law applied in a case is constitutional.

In some constitutional settings, the constitution or legislation or court rules permit constitutional challenges to be brought by people who are not directly affected by the legislation under challenge. The South African Constitution, for example, allows a person to act on behalf of another whose rights are affected but who is unable to act in their own name. It also permits, in special circumstances, a person acting in the public interest to initiate a constitutional challenge.[27] And in a growing number of jurisdictions, cases can be brought as class actions, where one litigant, or a group of them, may act on behalf of a larger class of people whose rights have all been adversely affected by the conduct of the defendant. When cases may be brought, and who may bring them, significantly affects the role played by courts in any particular body politic.

And finally, what remedies courts may order in the case of a finding of a breach of human rights affects the role courts play in protecting rights. Remedies will be determined, at least in part, by the way rights are protected in a particular jurisdiction. So, legislation that protects a particular right, for

[27] See section 38 of the South African Constitution, 1996.

example, legislation protecting data privacy, is likely to provide specific remedies for breach of the right. General bills of rights, whether legislated or constitutional, may have general remedy provisions that will ordinarily include public law forms of relief, such as injunctive and mandatory relief. In some jurisdictions, a range of novel forms of structural injunction has been employed in which courts direct government defendants to take action to remediate the rights infringements.[28] Damages for the infringement of rights are another important form of relief. Scholars have noted that the normative and theoretical underpinnings of damages for human rights remain underexplored, partly because remedies for human rights lie at the intersection of public and private law, and partly because human rights are relatively new to legal doctrine, particularly when compared to private law causes of action.[29] Whether damages should be seen only in compensatory terms, that is providing remedies for actual material harms, or also in vindicatory terms, is an important question, as is the question of whether there should be causes of action based on the constitutional or legislated bill of rights, or whether existing causes of action in tort or delict (or other civil remedies) should be the basis for relief.

These eight elements (whether rights are protected constitutionally or legislatively, which rights are protected, the

[28] See the discussion in Abram Chayes, 'The Role of the Judge in Public Law Litigation' (1976) 89 *Harvard Law Review* 1281–1316.

[29] See the discussion in Jason Varuhas, *Damages and Human Rights* (Hart, 2016), introduction, 1–10 and in Ugljesa Grusic and Ekaterina Aristova (eds.), *Civil Remedies and Human Rights in Flux: Key Legal Developments in Selected Jurisdictions* (Hart, 2022), introduction.

precise formulation of rights, the relationship between international law and domestic law, whether and how rights may be limited, how amendable rights protections are, in what circumstances courts may adjudicate alleged infringements of rights and what remedies are available for rights infringements) determine the role courts play in protecting rights and lead to significant variations between different constitutional frameworks.

Is There a Normative Argument to Be Made That Courts Should Be Conferred with a Role to Protect Rights?

In answering this question, we need to bear in mind the fundamental differences that exist between different bodies politic. It has been a key theme of this book that we should be circumspect about making general claims about the role of courts in the body politic that apply across all societies regardless of their different constitutional frameworks, different histories and different legal and political cultures. Yet, in one important respect, at least, it seems clear that this question should be decisively answered in the affirmative. For in all modern societies, legislation is a key mechanism for the protection of human rights.[30] Codes of criminal procedure, legislation regulating primary and secondary education and electoral laws are all examples of legislative mechanisms for

[30] See Gregoire Webber, Paul Yowell, Richard Ekins, Maris Köpcke, Bradley Miller and Francisco Urbina, *Legislated Rights: Securing Human Rights through Legislation* (Cambridge University Press, 2018).

the protection of human rights. Courts must interpret and apply these legislative mechanisms as they do all laws. When doing so they inevitably protect and fulfil human rights obligations.

The more contested and difficult question is whether it can be claimed that courts should be conferred with a broader responsibility for the protection of rights. There are two key mechanisms, discussed earlier, whereby courts can be given such a responsibility. The first mechanism is a constitutionally entrenched bill of rights, and the second is a legislated bill of rights. Both contain a catalogue of rights. The main difference is that a legislated bill of rights does not bind the legislature as constitutional bills of rights mostly do.

Scholars have termed the form of review under legislative bills of rights weak-form review, to distinguish it from strong-form review under entrenched bills of rights.[31] By and large, the primary criterion for whether review is strong or weak is whether courts can strike down legislation that they have held to be inconsistent with constitutional rights.[32] Aileen Kavanagh has questioned whether this distinction is

[31] See Stephen Gardbaum, *The New Commonwealth Model of Constitutionalism: Theory and Practice* (Cambridge University Press, 2013); Mark Tushnet, *Weak Courts, Strong Rights: Judicial Review and Social Welfare Rights in Comparative Constitutional Law* (Princeton University Press, 2009). Also see Richard Bellamy, 'Political Constitutionalism and the Human Rights Act' (2011) 9 *International Journal of Constitutional Law* 86–111.

[32] For different criteria for distinguishing weak- and strong-forms of review, see Stephen Gardbaum, 'Weak-Form Review in Comparative Perspective: A Reply' (2019) 17 *International Journal of Constitutional Law* 931–942.

helpful, noting, amongst other things, that the distinction detaches design from practice, and thus may obscure how judicial review actually works.[33] Although Kavanagh is right in alerting us to the importance of assessing and comparing how bills of rights work in practice rather than on paper, there is nevertheless an important difference in the role that courts are authorised to perform under a constitutional bill of rights that authorises courts to declare legislation invalid and a legislative bill of rights that does not.

Let us start with the question of whether courts should be conferred with the strong-form judicial review power to declare legislation that is inconsistent with the constitution invalid, as most written constitutions now do. There is a robust, and perennial, debate about strong-form judicial review: is it consistent with democracy to afford courts the power to declare legislation enacted by a democratic legislature to be invalid?

In an elegant and influential article, Jeremy Waldron argued that if four key assumptions hold, strong-form judicial review 'is inappropriate as a mode of final decision-making in a free and democratic society'.[34] He gives two reasons: firstly, he argues that judicial review distracts from core political disagreements about rights, instead focussing attention on precedent, text and interpretation. Secondly, he argues that

[33] See Aileen Kavanagh, 'What's So Weak about 'Weak-Form Review'? The Case of the UK Human Rights Act 1998' (2015) 13 *International Journal of Constitutional Law* 1008.

[34] Jeremy Waldron, 'The Core of the Case against Judicial Review' (2006) 115 *Yale Law Journal* 1346–1406.

judicial review 'disenfranchises ordinary citizens and brushes aside cherished principles of representation and political equality in the final resolution' of disagreements about rights.[35]

His argument at the level of democratic theory is intuitively attractive, but it is important to examine its four founding assumptions, which, in my view, undermine the reach and cogency of the argument. Waldron stipulates that his argument will obtain if (a) democratic institutions are in 'reasonably good working order' including a representative legislature elected on the basis of universal suffrage;[36] (b) judicial institutions are in reasonably good order, and are set up on a non-representative basis to hear and adjudicate disputes and uphold the rule of law;[37] (c) there is 'a commitment on the part of most members of the society and most of its officials to the idea of individual and minority rights';[38] and (d) there is 'persisting, substantial and good faith disagreement about rights'.[39]

For the argument to hold, these conditions need to exist not only when a constitutional framework is being adopted, but they also need to be likely to continue to exist in the future. There are not many societies in which these four conditions hold and probably none in which one can be certain that they will continue to do so. As importantly, however, given the circumstances in which constitutions are mostly adopted, the time of constitution-making will often be the least propitious time for the likely presence of Waldron's four conditions.

[35] Ibid., 1353. [36] Ibid., 1360. [37] Ibid. [38] Ibid. [39] Ibid.

In Chapter 1, I explored the circumstances under which modern constitutions have generally been adopted. They are often politically and social fraught. Many constitutions are adopted as peace agreements in post-conflict situations, or at the end of periods of imperial or colonial rule, or at the end of a war, or in times of transition from military or authoritarian rule. In such circumstances, national identity is often fragile and state formation incomplete or vulnerable. Democratic and judicial institutions will often be untested or undergoing transformation, and it will not be possible to say whether they are or will be, as Waldron puts it, 'in good working order'. And again, in these situations, it will often be difficult to assess whether there is a deep-seated commitment to upholding individual and minority rights and whether disagreement about rights will be reasonable or in good faith.[40] The moment when constitutions are made will thus rarely be a time when Waldron's four criteria will be clearly manifested.

Of course, it does not follow that if Waldron's four conditions do not hold, it will necessarily be appropriate to confer upon courts the power to exercise strong-form judicial review. The absence of Waldron's four conditions will simply mean that robust and good faith protection of rights by the legislature may be less reliable. It is that uncertainty that may lead constitutional drafters to favour strong-form review. Indeed, again as explored in Chapter 1, the decision to confer

[40] See the useful discussion in Scott Stephenson, 'Is the Commonwealth's Approach to Rights Constitutionalism Exportable?' (2019) 17 *International Journal of Constitutional Law* 884–903, 892.

strong-form review powers upon courts is often a political decision made at the time the constitution is made by political actors.[41] In an early influential study, Tom Ginsburg argued that politicians often see strong-form review as an insurance policy that will provide protection should they lose power in the years ahead, assuming that strong-form review may limit the ability of subsequent leaders to change the rules of the game. The fact that political leaders opt for strong-form review may thus be an indicator that they are not confident that Waldron's conditions will hold in their body politic, and they seek therefore to provide some guarantee of the endurance of the constitutional framework.

There is another argument for strong-form judicial review that warrants consideration. The genesis of this argument is in a footnote in a 1938 decision of the United States Supreme Court called *Carolene Products*.[42] The case was decided not long after a constitutional crisis concerning the US Supreme Court was narrowly averted. The crisis arose because in the early decades of the twentieth century, the US Supreme Court had delivered a series of decisions overturning social welfare legislation enacted by federal and state governments. This series of decisions has been named after a

[41] Tom Ginsburg, *Judicial Review in New Democracies: Constitutional Choices in Asian Cases* (Cambridge University Press, 2003). See also, Ran Hirschl, *Towards Juristocracy: The Origins and Consequences of the New Constitutionalism* (Harvard University Press, 2004); Ginsburg and Versteeg, n. 14; Tom Ginsburg and Rosalind Dixon, 'The Forms and Limits of Constitutions as Political Insurance' (2017) 15 *International Journal of Constitutional Law* 988–1012.

[42] See *United States v Carolene Products* 304 US 144 (1938), footnote 4.

1905 decision, *Lochner v New York*,[43] in which the Court held that New York legislation stipulating maximum hours of work infringed the Fourteenth Amendment to the Constitution.

The line of decisions that followed *Lochner* frustrated President Roosevelt who was seeking to implement his New Deal policies. And in February 1937, Roosevelt published a Judicial Procedures Reform Bill, which proposed to add more judges to the Supreme Court.[44] Just two months after the bill was published, the US Supreme Court issued a decision[45] in which one of the judges who had previously supported the Lochner line of reasoning changed his position to support those who had consistently opposed it. This moment is often referred to as the switch in time that saved nine.

Issued just a year later, *Carolene Products* concerned a constitutional challenge by a company accused of infringing a legislative scheme that prohibited the interstate shipment of skimmed milk compounded with other fats to resemble milk. The applicant argued that the legislation was unconstitutional for two reasons – because it exceeded congress' power to regulate interstate commerce and because it infringed the fifth amendment to the US Constitution, the property clause. The

[43] 198 US 45 (1905).

[44] The US Constitution does not stipulate the number of judges to serve on the Supreme Court and the number has varied. In 1869, the Judiciary Act provided that the court would consist of the chief justice and eight associate justices. Roosevelt's draft legislation proposed that he would appoint a new justice for every justice over the age of seventy who did not retire.

[45] *West Coast Hotel Co v Parrish* 300 US 379 (1937).

Court held that the legislation did not infringe either element of the constitutional framework and dismissed the challenge. In doing so, the Court held that the evidence received by congress when enacting the legislation was adequate but, it continued, even in the absence of evidence of an adequate rationale, the court would ordinarily presume legislation to have a rational basis. Accordingly, unless 'in the light of the facts made known or generally assumed it is of such a character as to preclude the assumption that it rests upon some rational basis within the knowledge and experience of the legislators', the court would not strike down a statute for want of an adequate rationale.[46]

This was a feather light-touch approach to strong-form judicial review – very different to the reasoning that had been prevalent during the *Lochner* era. Footnote 4 carved two possible qualifications from the conclusion of the court that it would presume an adequate rationale, unless there was reason on the record to suggest there was none. Those qualifications were formulated in these terms:

> It is unnecessary to consider now whether legislation which restricts those political processes which can ordinarily be expected to bring about repeal of undesirable legislation is to be subjected to more exacting judicial scrutiny . . . Nor need we enquire whether similar considerations enter into the review of statutes directed at particular religious, or national, or racial minorities, [or] whether prejudice against discrete and insular minorities may be a special condition, which tends seriously to curtail

[46] See *Carolene Products*, n. 42, para. 11.

> the operation of these political processes ordinarily to be relied upon to protect minorities, and which may call for a correspondingly more searching judicial enquiry.[47]

The footnote thus suggested that legislation aimed at restricting political processes or directed at discrete and insular minorities might warrant 'more exacting judicial scrutiny'. The footnote formed the basis for a very powerful defence of strong-form judicial review in these circumstances launched by US law professor, John Hart Ely. Ely argued that strong-form judicial review is legitimate where it protects the political process from inappropriate interference by political incumbents, and where it protects minority groups from discrimination. Accordingly, he argued that judges should adopt 'representation-reinforcing and participation-enhancing' jurisprudence to protect the democratic system.

Ely's two conditions for the legitimacy of strong-form review match two of the conditions that Waldron identified: Ely's argument is first that courts should act to preserve the good working order of the democratic institutions of government (Waldron's first condition, you will recall, was that democratic institutions should be in good working order) and second that courts should act to protect vulnerable minorities against discrimination by the majority (Waldron's third condition was that most members of society, and most officials, should be committed to the idea of individual and minority rights). Ely's account therefore carves out a legitimate role for constitutional review to ensure that

[47] Ibid.

Waldron's first condition is maintained and to provide protection to minorities when his third condition is not met.

Ely's process-based account of strong-form judicial review is enjoying a renaissance in the current global context, where, as I outlined in both Chapters 1 and 2, we are seeing a pattern of democratic regression in many democracies across the world.[48] Stephen Gardbaum has argued that the central insight of a political process theory of judicial review is that 'protection of a system of representative democracy against erosion or degradation by elected representatives cannot be left exclusively in their hands'.[49] Gardbaum argues that Ely's approach should be expanded to include all the processes 'through which public power is allocated, exercised and held to account'.[50] Thus, a political process theory of judicial review could address two of the greatest risks to a democracy – firstly,

[48] See, for example, Stephen Gardbaum, 'Comparative Political Process Theory' (2020) 18 *International Journal of Constitutional Law* 1429–1457; Doreen Lustig and Joseph H. H. Weiler, 'Judicial Review in the Contemporary World: Retrospective and Prospective' (2018) 16 *International Journal of Constitutional Law* 315–372; Sergio Verdugo, 'Limited Democracy and Great Distrust: John Hart Ely in Bolivia and Chile' (2021) 19 *International Journal of Constitutional Law* 515–532; Rosalind Dixon, *Responsive Judicial Review* (Oxford University Press, 2022); David Landau, 'Political Institutions and Judicial Role in Comparative Constitutional Law' (2010) 51 *Harvard International Law Journal* 320–377; Firoz Cachalia, 'Precautionary Constitutionalism, Representative Democracy and Political Corruption' (2019) 9 *Constitutional Court Review* 45–80; Jacob Rowbottom, 'Political Purposes, Anti-Entrenchment and Judicial Protection of the Democratic Process' (2022) 42 *Oxford Journal of Legal Studies* 383–410.

[49] See Gardbaum, n. 48, 1430. See also Dixon, n. 48.

[50] Gardbaum, n. 48, 1431.

that an incumbent government will change the rules of the game to prevent a handover of power; and secondly, the risk that majoritarian governments may seek to discriminate against vulnerable minorities.

A political process account of strong-form judicial review is intuitively attractive but as with many intuitively attractive accounts, its greatest challenge lies in the details of its application. In a thoughtful recent article assessing the impact of Ely in Germany, Michaela Hailbronner concluded that when courts intervene in democracy there is a risk that they may do more harm than good. If we are to develop a workable and defensible political process theory, Hailbronner says, we need to be able to address three questions: how should courts determine whether existing processes are malfunctioning, and why they are not working well. And once we are satisfied with how to answer these questions, the further question of what remedies courts should order remains.[51]

In summary, I draw several conclusions in answering the question of whether courts should be conferred with the power to protect rights. First, there can be no doubt that courts in modern democracies should be engaged in protecting human rights, where those protections are contained in legislation directed at the protection of specific rights. Such legislation provides an important mechanism for the protection of rights in all jurisdictions and should be implemented by courts.

[51] See Michaela Hailbronner, 'Combatting Malfunction or Optimising Democracy? Lessons from Germany for a Comparative Political Process Theory' (2021) 19 *International Journal of Constitutional Law* 495–514.

Second, the enactment of legislative bills of rights confers courts with the role of protecting human rights. Even those firmly opposed to strong-form review, generally accept that weak-form review under a legislative bill of rights is not incompatible with democracy. Richard Bellamy, a leading opponent of strong-form constitutional review, takes the view that the UK HRA strikes an appropriate balance between protecting the democratic role of parliament and ensuring the protection of rights.[52]

Third, strong-form judicial review of legislation for rights compatibility raises more difficult questions to answer for all societies in all circumstances. I have explained that given the circumstances in which most modern constitutions are written, it will rarely be certain that Waldron's four criteria upon which his core case against judicial review is founded exist (and will continue to exist) at the moment of constitutional entrenchment. Uncertainty about whether the democratic institutions will work well under the new framework, whether there will be an enduring commitment to individual and minority rights and whether disagreement about rights will be articulated in good faith will often lead constitutional drafters to consider including strong-form judicial review in the constitutional design. Where a constitutional text does explicitly confer strong-form judicial review upon courts, courts are obliged in good faith and with fidelity to law to exercise those powers. Of course, in practice, courts' performance of their role under strong-form review may be less than ideal. And where courts get things wrong in a

52 See Bellamy, n. 31. See also Webber et al., n. 30, 153.

strong-form constitutional review framework it is often hard to put things right. In these circumstances, no general claim that strong-form judicial review is always appropriate for the protection of rights can be made. Yet, we might say that the case for it is at its strongest where many, if not all, of the following circumstances are present:

- in divided and unequal societies in which groups might be at particular risk of majority abuse;
- where the courts are seen as independent and impartial;
- there is both an independent and competent legal profession and an engaged legal academy where good training is provided to lawyers;
- there is a constitutional text, which is reasonably capable of amendment, adopted following a fair and inclusive democratic process, in which the power of judicial review is explicitly provided; and
- which adopts a two-stage model for the adjudication of rights, which recognises that rights may be limited where government can show that it is reasonable and justifiable to do so.[53]

Given that I have concluded that it is not inappropriate for courts to adjudicate legislative bills of rights, it is appropriate now to turn to the perennial debate in the United Kingdom about the HRA.

[53] See Kate O'Regan, 'Contemporary Challenges for Human Rights: A View from South Africa' in Simon Mount and Max Harris (eds.), *The Promise of Law: Essays Marking the Retirement of Chief Justice Sian Elias* (Lexis Nexis, 2020).

The UK HRA Debate

The current government in the United Kingdom has repeatedly expressed its concern about the role that courts play in protecting rights in the United Kingdom. The HRA gives domestic effect to the rights contained in the ECHR, which was drafted not long after the adoption of the UDHR. Famously, British lawyers played a key role in the drafting of the ECHR.

Between 1950 and 1998, when the HRA came into force, British courts had no jurisdiction to entertain claims based on the ECHR, and people who wished to rely on the rights in the ECHR had to go to the European Court of Human Rights in Strasbourg. The HRA changed that. The White Paper that introduced it spoke of 'bringing rights home' and ensuring that British courts could, at last, adjudicate the rights in the EHCR.[54] Yet, it is noteworthy that the adoption of the HRA did not settle ongoing controversy about the role of the ECHR in British law. As Lord Carnwath, a former judge of the Supreme Court, observed in a recent lecture, 'I cannot remember a time when the place of the [European] Convention in our law has not been a subject of active debate.'[55]

[54] See *Rights Brought Home: The Human Rights Bill* (October 1997, CM 3782).

[55] See Lord Carnwath, 'Is It Time for a New British Bill of Rights?' delivered 9 February 2022, Cambridge, available at https://constitutionallawmatters.org/2022/02/09/lord-carnwath-lecture-on-human-rights-act-reform-is-it-time-for-a-new-british-bill-of-rights/ (last accessed on 27 March 2024).

The key operative provisions of the HRA are: firstly, people who allege an infringement of one of the rights under the ECHR may now approach British courts for a remedy. Secondly, the Act provides that when courts decide questions concerned with convention rights, they should 'take into account' the jurisprudence of the ECHR.[56]

When the then lord chancellor, Lord Irvine, introduced the Human Rights Bill to parliament, he stated that the Act would permit UK courts to depart from Strasbourg decisions,[57] and British courts have recognised that although ordinarily they should follow Strasbourg, if there are strong reasons to do so, they may depart from Strasbourg jurisprudence.[58]

Thirdly, the Act provides that when interpreting legislation, British courts should 'so far as it is possible to do so' interpret legislation in a manner that will give effect to convention rights.[59] The UK courts have taken a broad approach to this mandate – recognising that at times it may require courts to 'depart from the unambiguous meaning the legislation would otherwise bear'.[60] This has been controversial but the interpretive provision in some senses is the twin of the fourth key operative provision in the Act, which provides that when a court concludes that a legislative provision cannot be read in a manner compatible with convention

[56] HRA, section 2.

[57] See 583 HL 514, 515 (8 November 1987); 584 HL col 1271, cited in Aileen Kavanagh, *Constitutional Review under the UK Human Rights Act* (CambridgeUniversity Press, 2009), 407.

[58] See *R (Ullah) v Special Adjudicator* [2004] UKHL 26.

[59] HRA, section 3.

[60] See *Ghaidan v Godin-Mendoza* [2004] UKHL 30.

rights, it may choose to issue a declaration of incompatibility.[61] As mentioned above, the declaration of incompatibility does not affect the validity of the provision, but the effect of the declaration is to draw the issue to the attention of parliament.

Declarations of incompatibility are infrequent: in the twenty years between 2000 and 2020, declarations were issued only forty-three times.[62] Nine of these declarations were overturned on appeal, five related to provisions that had already been amended by the time of the declaration, fifteen have been addressed by primary or secondary legislation and a further eight have been addressed by remedial order and the remainder are either subject to appeal, been addressed in another way, or under consideration by government.[63] In her careful analysis of parliamentary responses to declarations of incompatibility, Aileen Kavanagh concludes that only four generated 'heated political debate and resistance'.[64]

[61] See HRA, section 4.

[62] Ministry of Justice, *Responding to Human Rights Judgments: Report to the Joint Committee on Human Rights on the Government Response to Human Rights Judgments, 2019–2020*, p. 29.

[63] See the Independent Human Rights Act Review Report (December 2021), paras. 92–93, available at https://assets.publishing.service.gov.uk/government/uploads/system/uploads/attachment_data/file/1040525/ihrar-final-report.pdf (last accessed on 27 March 2024).

[64] See Aileen Kavanagh, *The Collaborative Constitution* (Cambridge University Press, 2023), ch. 12. I am grateful to Aileen for providing me with an advance copy of her book. The four controversial examples were *Anderson*, which found that the home secretary's involvement in sentencing violated article 6; the *Belmarsh Prison* case, which declared that executive detention without trial of non-national suspects violated

She also concludes that parliamentary committees have generally treated declarations as 'authoritative judicial rulings they are obliged to respect' and that the response has been 'predominantly collaborative rather than conflictual'.[65]

In December 2020, the then Lord Chancellor and Secretary of State for Justice Robert Buckland, announced the establishment of an independent review into the HRA, to be chaired by retired Court of Appeal judge, Sir Peter Gross. The terms of reference requested the panel to explore two key themes, the relationship between the British courts and the ECHR, and the impact of the HRA on the relationship between the executive, legislature and judiciary in the United Kingdom. A firm premise of the review was that government was not contemplating withdrawal from the ECHR. The review was focussed, not on the substantive rights in the ECHR, but on how the HRA worked. The panel adopted an open and inclusive process: calling for evidence and responses from individuals and organisations, hosting fourteen online roundtables, as well as seven online 'roadshows' facilitated by universities.[66] The panel issued its careful and comprehensive report in October 2021. By and large, the review concluded that the HRA was working well, but it recommended a few modest changes to the legislation to clarify and refine it.

the right to non-discrimination; the *Thompson* case, which found that placing sex offenders on a register indefinitely without possible right of review violated privacy; and *Smith v Scott*, on prisoner voting, which followed the ruling in *Hirst*, the first prisoner voting case. See also the Ministry of Justice report, n. 62.

[65] Kavanagh, n. 64. [66] IHRAR, n. 63, annexure 7.

On the same day that the Independent Human Rights Act Review Report (IHRAR) was published,[67] the government issued a consultation paper in which it invited comments on proposals to revise and replace the HRA with a UK bill of rights. The consultation raised twenty-nine questions for which comments were invited. As Sir Peter Gross, the chair of the independent review, observed in his evidence to the Justice Committee in February 2022, the consultation paper was not a response to the panel's report. It appeared to be an entirely different project.

That it was became clear when, following the consultation paper, the government published a bill of rights bill on 22 June 2022. The bill proposed the repeal of the HRA and the enactment of a legislative bill of rights. The government sought to fast-track the bill through parliament. Just over a week after the first reading of the bill, on 30 June 2022, the acting chair of the Joint Committee on Human Rights (a committee responsible for scrutinising the government's human rights record, comprising members of both the Commons and the Lords) wrote to the lord chancellor to express concerns, noting that the inquiries conducted by the Joint Committee for Human Rights (JCHR) had led the Committee to conclude that the HRA is functioning as intended, enabling human rights to be enforced effectively in the United Kingdom with little recourse required to the European Court of Human Rights.[68]

[67] 14 December 2021.

[68] The letter is available on the website of the JCHR here: https://committees.parliament.uk/publications/22880/documents/167940/

The letter drew attention to the evidence the committee had received from Judge Robert Spano, the president of the European Court of Human Rights,[69] who noted that since 2017, the United Kingdom, of all the forty-seven member states of the Council of Europe, had the lowest number of cases pending before the Court. Between 301 and 415 applications against the United Kingdom were filed between 2017 and 2021, which is between 0.04 and 0.06 applications per capita. In January 2021, there were in total 62,000 cases pending before the European Court of Human Rights, of which 124 were related to the United Kingdom. Judge Spano also noted that the vast majority of cases brought against the United Kingdom are dismissed by the ECHR as inadmissible. In 2020, for example, the Court decided 284 cases in which the United Kingdom was a respondent. It dismissed as inadmissible 280 of these, found no violation in one case, a friendly settlement was struck in another and found against the United Kingdom in only two cases.

The second reading of the draft bill of rights was postponed in early September 2022 after Liz Truss became prime minister following the leadership contest in the Conservative Party during the summer and the minister

default/ (last accessed on 27 March 2024). See also the subsequent report of the JCHR, *Legislative Scrutiny: Bill of Rights Bill Report*, dated 17 January 2023, available here https://committees.parliament.uk/publications/33649/documents/183913/default/ (last accessed on 27 March 2024).

69 See evidence of Judge Robert Spano before the JCHR, dated 17 February 2021, available online here https://committees.parliament.uk/writtenevidence/22906/pdf/ (last accessed on 1 October 2022).

responsible for its introduction, Dominic Raab, left the cabinet. However, following the election of Rishi Sunak as prime minister, Dominic Raab once again returned to the cabinet and it was announced that the Bill of Rights bill would once again come before parliament. However, that did not happen.[70]

The abandonment of the Bill of Rights bill does not mean that the political contestation around the role of courts in the protection of rights in the United Kingdom has abated. The Bill of Rights bill did not propose that the United Kingdom withdraw from the ECHR, yet there is little doubt that the question of United Kingdom's continued membership of the Council of Europe and its ratification of the ECHR remains a contested issue within the Conservative Party. During the public debates at the time of the leadership contest in the summer of 2022, several senior members of the Conservative Party suggested that the way forward was to withdraw from the ECHR. As an outsider, and someone who comes from a post-conflict society, in which the entrenchment of human rights is by and large an uncontroversial matter, the debate in the United Kingdom about its membership of the ECHR is both puzzling and disquieting.

The debate is puzzling because the HRA in Britain represents an adept accommodation of two conflicting principles: democracy and respect for human rights. And even those political theorists most sceptical of constitutional review

[70] On 27 June 2023, Alex Chalk, the then vice chancellor and secretary of state for justice informed the House of Commons that the government had decided not to proceed with the Bill of Rights bill.

respect the balance struck in the HRA. Opposition to it, therefore, cannot easily be explained as a democratic concern. Parliament remains sovereign in the law that it chooses to make and unmake.

It seems to me that much of the scepticism concerning the protection of human rights in Britain properly understood is not scepticism about the design of the HRA and that is disquieting. For it appears to be scepticism about the regional (and international) project that seeks to ensure the protection of human rights for all which I described at the outset of this chapter. Today the divide between illiberal and authoritarian societies who in their deeds, if not their words, scorn the international human rights project, and those societies that remain committed to the post-Second World War vision of a commitment to international human rights, as the foundation of freedom, justice and peace in the world, is deepening. It is a worrying time for societies who have been committed to human rights to be wavering in their commitment to the global protection of human rights.

Conclusion

In summary, this book has suggested that the role courts play in modern bodies politic has expanded significantly as a result of the practice of writing constitutions, either as big-C constitutions or in legislation of constitutional significance as in Northern Ireland and Brexit. Constitution-writing often takes place in difficult and contested circumstances, and it is these circumstances that have informed the decision to expand the role of courts. That expansion has often been driven by political actors seeking to ensure the endurance of a constitution in circumstances of fragility and uncertainty. In understanding the role that courts play in any constitutional framework, we need to recognise that courts are institutions within the broader body politic, which comprises not only the branches and institutions of the state but also actors, often characterised as private institutions, such as political parties, the media, civil society and the legal profession. How courts perform the roles conferred upon them by a constitutional framework depends not only on the legal and institutional culture of the court but also upon the institutions, relationships and culture of the broader body politic.

Given the factors that underpin the expanded role of courts in modern societies, the factors that determine how courts function and the spreading global pattern of democratic decline, responding to the expanded role of courts with a simple normative claim that it is democratically inappropriate for courts to perform these roles is unsatisfactory. Such claims often reflect an idealised account of how politics works, coupled with a failure to grasp the fragile and precarious character of the body politic in many modern societies. Insofar as the protection of human rights is concerned, courts always have an important role to play, although the precise boundaries of that role will vary depending on the character of the body politic of which they form part. Finally, it is always important to remember that courts are not the only institution that bears the responsibility to protect rights. If the legislature and executive turn firmly against the protection of rights, the ability of courts to assure them will be severely diminished, if not extinguished. The assertion of the UDHR that the recognition of the equal and inalienable rights of all were the foundation of justice, peace and security in the world remains as timely and important in 2022 as it was in 1947. Courts have a role to play in the protection of rights, but it is not their responsibility alone. It is a responsibility borne by all in the body politic.

SELECT BIBLIOGRAPHY

Ackerman, Bruce, 'The Emergency Constitution', 113 (2004) *Yale Law Journal* 1029

We the People, Volume 1: Foundations (Harvard University Press, 1993)

We the People, Volume 2: Transformations (Harvard University Press, 2000)

We the People, Volume 3: The Civil Rights Revolution (Harvard University Press, 2018)

Agamben, Giorgio, *State of Exception* (University of Chicago Press, 2005)

Aristotle, *Politics*, Book 3, 1281b

Bagenholm, Andreas, 'Throwing the Rascals Out? The Electoral Effects of Corruption Allegations and Corruption Scandals in Europe' (2013) 60 *Crime, Law and Social Change* 595–609.

Barber, N. W. (ed.), *The Principles of Constitutionalism* (Oxford University Press, 2018)

Barendt, E. 'Separation of Powers and Constitutional Government' [1995] *Public Law* 599

Baum, Lawrence, *Judges and Their Audiences: A Perspective on Judicial Behavior* (Princeton University Press, 2008)

Bellamy, Richard, 'Political Constitutionalism and the Human Rights Act' (2011) 9 *International Journal of Constitutional Law* 86–111

Bermeo, Nancy, 'On Democratic Backsliding' (2016) 27 *Journal of Democracy* 4–19

Bhuwania, Anuj, *Courting the People: Public Interest Litigation in Post-Emergency India* (Cambridge University Press, 2017)

Bickel, Alexander, *The Least Dangerous Branch: The Supreme Court at the Bar of Politics* (Bobbs-Merrill, 1962)

Bjornskov, Christian and Stefan Voigt, 'The Architecture of Emergency Constitutions' (2018) 16 *International Journal of Constitutional Law* 101–127

Cachalia, Firoz, 'Precautionary Constitutionalism, Representative Democracy and Political Corruption' (2019) 9 *Constitutional Court Review* 45–81

Lord Carnwath, 'Is It Time for a New British Bill of Rights?' delivered 9 February 2022, Cambridge, available at https://constitutionallawmatters.org/2022/02/09/lord-carnwath-lecture-on-human-rights-act-reform-is-it-time-for-a-new-british-bill-of-rights/ (last accessed on 27 March 2024).

Chanock, Martin, *The Making of South African Legal Culture, 1902–1936: Fear, Favour and Prejudice* (Cambridge University Press, 2001)

Chayes, Abram, 'The Role of the Judge in Public Law Litigation' (1976) 89 *Harvard Law Review* 1281–1316

Cohn, Margit, *A Theory of the Executive Branch: Tension and Legality* (Oxford University Press, 2021)

Colley, Linda, *The Gun, the Ship and the Pen: Warfare, Constitutions and the Making of the Modern World* (Profile Books, 2021)

Covington, Sarah, *Wounds, Flesh and Metaphor in Seventeenth-Century England* (Palgrave Macmillan, 2009)

Craig, Paul and Adam Tomkins, *The Executive and Public Law: Power and Accountability in Comparative Perspective* (Oxford University Press, 2005)

Deb, Anurag, 'The Union in Court: *Allister and Others' Application for Judicial Review* [2021] NIQB 64' (2022) 73(1) *Northern Ireland Legal Quarterly* 138–161

Diamond, Larry, 'Facing Up to the Democratic Recession' (2015) 26 *Journal of Democracy* 141

Dicey, A. V., *Introduction to the Law of the Constitution* (Macmillan, 1915)

Dixon, Rosalind, *Responsive Judicial Review* (Oxford University Press, 2022)

Dixon, Rosalind and David Landau, 'Tiered Constitutional Design' (2018) 86 *George Washington Law Review* 438–512

Dyzenhaus, David, *The Constitution of Law: Legality in a Time of Emergency* (Cambridge University Press, 2006)

Elkins, Zachary and Tom Ginsburg, 'Imagining a World without the Universal Declaration of Human Rights' 74 (2022) *World Politics* 327–366

Elkins, Zachary, Tom Ginsburg and Beth Simmons, 'Getting to Rights: Treaty Ratification, Constitutional Convergence and Human Rights Practice' (2013) 54 *Harvard International Law Journal* 61–96

Ferejohn, John and Pasquale Pasquino, 'The Law of the Exception: A Typology of Emergency Powers' (2004) 2 *International Journal of Constitutional Law* 210–239

Fukuyama, Francis, 'The End of History?' (1989) 16 *The National Interest* 3–18

Fuller, Lon L., 'The Forms and Limits of Adjudication' (1978) 92 *Harvard Law Review* 364

Gal, Andras, 'Beyond "Unwinding": Constitutional Review Strategies in Consociations' (2020) 26 *Nations and Nationalism* 594–610

Gardbaum, Stephen, 'Comparative Political Process Theory' (2020) 18 *International Journal of Constitutional Law* 1429–1457

The New Commonwealth Model of Constitutionalism: Theory and Practice (Cambridge University Press, 2013)

'Pushing the Boundaries; Judicial Review of Legislative Procedures in South Africa' (2019) 9 *Constitutional Court Review* 1–18

'Weak-Form Review in Comparative Perspective: A Reply' (2019) 17 *International Journal of Constitutional Law* 931–942

Ginsburg, Tom, *Judicial Review in New Democracies: Constitutional Choices in Asian Cases* (Cambridge University Press, 2003)

Ginsburg, Tom and Ros Dixon, 'The Forms and Limits of Constitutions as Political Insurance' (2017) 15 *International Journal of Constitutional Law* 988–1012

Ginsburg, Tom and Aziz Huq, 'How to Lose a Constitutional Democracy' (2018) 65 *University of California Law Review* 78

How to Save a Constitutional Democracy (University of Chicago Press, 2018)

Ginsburg, Tom and Aziz Huq (eds.), *From Parchment to Practice, Implementing New Constitutions* (Cambridge University Press, 2020)

Ginsburg, Tom and James Melton, 'Does the Constitutional Amendment Rule Matter at All?' (2015) 13 *International Journal of Constitutional Law* 686–713

Ginsburg, Tom and Mila Versteeg, 'States of Emergencies: Part 1' *Harvard Law Review Blog*, 17 April 2020

'Why Do Countries Adopt Constitutional Review?' (2013) 30 *Journal of Law, Economics and Organisation* 587–622

Graber, Mark A., 'What's in Crisis? The Postwar Constitutional Paradigm, Transformative Constitutionalism and the Fate of Constitutional Democracy' in Mark A. Graber, Sanford Levinson and Mark Tushnet (eds.), *Constitutional Democracy in Crisis?* (Oxford University Press, 2018)

Hadfield, Gillian, Jens Meierhenrich and Barry Weingast, 'A Positive Theory of the Rule of Law' in Jens Meierhenrich and Martin Loughlin (eds.), *The Cambridge Companion to the Rule of Law* (Cambridge University Press, 2021)

Hailbronner, Michaela, 'Combatting Malfunction or Optimising Democracy? Lessons from Germany for a Comparative Political Process Theory' (2021) 19 *International Journal of Constitutional Law* 495–514

Traditions and Transformations: The Rise of German Constitutionalism (Oxford University Press, 2016)

Hamilton, Alexander, *The Federalist No. 70*, 15 March 1788

The Federalist No. 78, 28 May 1788

Hendley, Kathryn, *Everyday Law in Russia* (Cornell University Press, 2017)

Hilbink, Lisa, *Judges beyond Politics in Democracy and Dictatorship: Lessons from Chile* (Cambridge University Press, 2007)

Hirschl, Ran, *Towards Juristocracy: The Origins and Consequences of the New Constitutionalism* (Harvard University Press, 2004)

Hobsbawm, Eric, 'Introduction' in Eric Hobsbawm and Terence Ranger (eds.), *The Invention of Tradition* (Cambridge University Press, 2012, first published 1983)

Huntington, Samuel, *The Third Wave: Democratisation in the Late Twentieth Century* (University of Oklahoma, 1993)

Huq, Aziz, 'A Tactical Separation of Powers Doctrine' (2019) 9 *Constitutional Court Review* 19–44

Issacharoff, Samuel, *Fragile Democracies: Contested Power in the Era of Constitutional Courts* (Cambridge University Press, 2015)

Jakab, Andras, Arthur Dyevre and Giulio Itzcovich (eds.), *Comparative Constitutional Reasoning* (Cambridge University Press, 2017)

Jensen, Steven, *The Making of International Human Rights: The 1960s, Decolonization and the Reconstruction of Global Values* (Cambridge University Press, 2016)

Johnston, Michael, 'How Do I Vote the Scoundrels Out? Why Voters Might Not Punish Corrupt Politicians at the Polls' (2013) 60 *Crime, Law and Social Change* 503–514

Kahn, Paul W., 'Constitutional Culture: Opening a Space between Law and Power' (2019) 189 *Telos* 15–33

Kavanagh, Aileen, *The Collaborative Constitution* (Cambridge University Press, 2023)

'What's So Weak about 'Weak-Form Review'? The Case of the UK Human Rights Act 1998' (2015) 13 *International Journal of Constitutional Law* 1008

'The Constitutional Separation of Powers' in D. Dyzenhaus and M. Thorburn (eds.), *Philosophical Foundations of Constitutional Law* (Oxford University Press, 2016)

Kössler, Karl, *Comparative Federalism: Constitutional Arrangements and Case Law* (Hart Publishing, 2017)

Krygier, Martin, 'Law as Tradition' (1986) 5 *Law and Philosophy* 237–262

Landau, David, 'Political Institutions and Judicial Role in Comparative Constitutional Law' (2010) 51 *Harvard International Law Journal* 320–377

Law, David, 'Constitutions' in Peter Cane and Herbert Kritzer (eds.), *Oxford Handbook of Empirical Legal Research* (Oxford University Press, 2010)

Law, David and Mila Versteeg, 'Sham Constitutions' (2013) 101 *California Law Review* 862–952

Lazar, Nomi Claire, *States of Emergency in Liberal Democracies* (Cambridge University Press, 2009)

Levitsky, Steven and Daniel Ziblatt, *How Democracies Die: What History Reveals about Our Future* (Penguin, 2018)

Livius (Livy), Titus, Book 2, *History of Rome*, ch. 32

Loughlin, Martin, *Against Constitutionalism* (Harvard University Press, 2022)

Lustig, Doreen and Joseph H. H. Weiler, 'Judicial Review in the Contemporary World: Retrospective and Prospective' (2018) 16 *International Journal of Constitutional Law* 315–372

Lutz, Ellen and Caitlin Reiger, *Prosecuting Heads of State* (Cambridge University Press, 2009)

Macchiavelli, Niccolò, *Discourses on Livy, ch.* 34 (1517)

Madison, James, *The Federalist*, No. 48, 1 February 1788

Mazower, Mark, 'The Strange Triumph of Human Rights, 1933–1950' (2004) 47 *The Historical Journal* 379–398

Möllers, C., *The Three Branches: A Comparative Model of the Separation of Powers* (Oxford University Press, 2013).

Montesquieu, C., *The Spirit of the Laws*, Book 11, ch. 6 and Book 19

Moravcsik, Andrew, 'The Origins of Human Rights Regimes: Democratic Delegation in Postwar Europe' (2000) 54 *International Organisation* 217–272

Mota Prado, Mariana and Marta R. de Assis Machado, 'Using Criminal Law to Fight Corruption: The Potentials, Risks and Limitations of Operation Car Wash' (2021) 69 *American Journal of Comparative Law* 834–87

Moustafa, Tamir, 'Law and Resistance in Authoritarian States: The Judicialization of Politics in Egypt' in Tamir Moustafa and Tom Ginsburg (eds.), *Rule by Law: The Politics of Courts in Authoritarian Regimes* (Cambridge University Press, 2008)

Mudde, Cas, 'The Populist Zeitgeist' (2004) 39 *Government and Opposition* 543

Musolff, Andreas, *Metaphor, Nation and the Holocaust: The Concept of the Body Politic* (Routledge, 2010)

'Political Metaphor and Bodies Politic' in U. Okulska and P. Cap (eds.), *Perspectives in Politics and Discourse* (John Benjamins, 2010)

Nederman, Cary J., and Kate Langdon Forhan (eds.), *Medieval Political Theory: A Reader – The Quest for the Body Politic* (Routledge, 1993)

Nelken, David, 'Comparative Legal Research and Legal Culture: Facts, Approaches and Values' (2016) 12 *Annual Review of Law and Society* 45–62

O'Leary, Brendan, *A Treatise on Northern Ireland, Volume III: Consociation and Confederation* (Oxford University Press, 2019)

O'Regan, Kate, 'Contemporary Challenges for Human Rights: A View from South Africa' in Simon Mount and Max Harris (eds.), *The Promise of Law: Essays Marking the Retirement of Chief Justice Sian Elias* (Lexis Nexis, 2020)

Pildes, Richard, 'Law and the President' (2012) 125 *Harvard Law Review* 1381–1424.

Popova, Maria, *Politicised Justice in Emerging Democracies: A Study of Courts in Russia and Ukraine* (Cambridge University Press, 2012)

Posner, Eric and Adrian Vermeule, *The Executive Unbound: After the Madisonian Republic* (Oxford University Press, 2011)

Posner, Richard, *Not a Suicide Pact: The Constitution in a Time of National Emergency* (Oxford University Press, 2006)

Public Protector of South Africa, *State of Capture: Report of an Investigation into Alleged Improper and Unethical Conduct by the President and Other State Functionaries relating to Alleged Improper Relationships and Involvement of the Gupta Family in the Removal and Appointment of Ministers and Directors off State-Owned Enterprises regulating in Improper and Possibly Corrupt Award of State Contracts and Benefits to the Gupta's Family Businesses* (Public Protector, South Africa, Report 6 of 2016/2017) dated 14 October 2016. Available at www.gov.za/sites/default/files/gcis_document/201611/stateofcapturereport14october2016_1.pdf

Rehnquist, William H., *All the Laws but One: Civil Liberties in Wartime* (Vintage Books, 2000)

Rose-Ackerman, Susan and Bonnie J. Palifka, *Corruption and Government: Causes, Consequences and Reform*, 2nd ed. (Cambridge University Press, 2016)

Rossiter, Clinton L., *Constitutional Dictatorship: Crisis Government in the Modern Democracies* (Princeton University Press, 1948)

Roux, Theunis, *The Politico-Legal Dynamics of Judicial Review: A Comparative Analysis* (Cambridge University Press, 2018)

Rowbottom, Jacob, 'Political Purposes, Anti-Entrenchment and Judicial Protection of the Democratic Process' (2022) 42 *Oxford Journal of Legal Studies* 383–410

Sadurski, Wojciech, *Poland's Constitutional Breakdown* (Oxford University Press, 2019)

Sberna, Salvatore and Alberto Vannucci, 'It's the Politics, Stupid! The Politicisation of Anti-Corruption in Italy' (2013) 60 *Crime Law and Society* 565–594

Schmitt, Carl, *Political Theology: Four Chapters on the Concept of Sovereignty* (University of Chicago Press, 2005, first published 1922)

Shapiro, Martin, *Courts: A Comparative and Political Analysis* (University of Chicago Press, 1981)

Smith, Sophie, 'Democracy and the Body Politic from Aristotle to Hobbes' (2018) 46 *Political Theory* 167–196

Stephenson, Scott, 'Is the Commonwealth's Approach to Rights Constitutionalism Exportable?' (2019) 17 *International Journal of Constitutional Law* 884–903

Sunstein, Cass, 'Minimalism at War' [2004] *The Supreme Court Review* 47–109

Tushnet, Mark, 'Institutions Supporting Constitutional Democracy: Some Thoughts about Anti-corruption' (2019) *Singapore Journal of Legal Studies* 440–455

Weak Courts, Strong Rights: Judicial Review and Social Welfare Rights in Comparative Constitutional Law (Princeton University Press, 2009)

Varuhas, Jason, *Damages and Human Rights* (Hart Publishing, 2016)

Verdugo, Sergio, 'Limited Democracy and Great Distrust: John Hart Ely in Bolivia and Chile' (2021) 19 *International Journal of Constitutional Law* 515–532

Waldron, Jeremy, 'The Core of the Case against Judicial Review' (2006) 115 *Yale Law Journal* 1346–1406

Political Political Theory (Harvard University Press, 2016)

Walters, Brian, *The Deaths of the Republic: Imagery of the Body Politic in Ciceronian Rome* (Oxford University Press, 2020)

Webber, Gregoire, Paul Yowell, Richard Ekins, Maris Köpcke, Bradley Miller and Francisco Urbina, *Legislated Rights: Securing Human Rights through Legislation* (Cambridge University Press, 2018)

Weiss, Avi, 'Binding the Bound: State Executive Emergency Powers and Democratic Legitimacy in the Pandemic' (2021) 121 *Columbia Law Review* 1853–1894

Widner, Jennifer, 'Constitution Writing in Post-Conflict Settings: An Overview' (2008) 49 *William and Mary Law Review* 1513–1542

INDEX

absolute rights, 85–86
accountability
  institutions, 16
  mechanisms, 48–52, 64–65, 72
Ackerman, Bruce, 21
address, modes, 2
adjudication
  definition, 41
  models, 44–45
administrators, 47
African Charter on Human and Peoples' Rights, 77, 85
amendability, 87
American Convention on Human Rights, 77, 85
apex courts, 40
appointment of judges, 43
Aristotle, 13
audience, 42
authoritarianism, 53–57

Belfast Agreement. *See* Good Friday Agreement
Bellamy, Richard, 101
Bermeo, Nancy, 11
bills of rights, 80–81, 85–87, 89, 91–92
  legislative, 101
Bingham, Lord, 27–28
Bjornskov, Christian, 59–60
body politic, metaphor, 13–17, 73–74
Brexit, 30–31
Buckland, Robert, 106
bureaucrats, 47

Canadian Charter of Rights and Freedoms, 83
Carnwath, Lord, 103
Chanock, Martin, 17
civil liberties, 63
civil servants, 47
Cohn, Margit, 51–52
Colley, Linda, 19–21
comparison, challenge of, 17–19
Constitute project, 19
Constitutional Court of South Africa, 1–6, 35–37
constitutional culture, 35
constitutional moments, 21
constitutionalism
  characteristics, 8
  spread, 7
constitution-making, 26
  conditions, 21–23
constitutions
  sham, 32
  South African, 84
  written, 80
    spread, 19–21
corruption, 63–72

corruption, (cont.)
definition, 63
counter-majoritarian dilemma, 7
courts
functional characteristics, 39–45
relationship with executive branch, 38, 72
roles in modern constitutional settings, 24–31
expanded, 31–37
COVID-19 pandemic, 60
Craig, Paul, 45
crises, 57–63
culture, 34

damages, for infringement of rights, 89
democracy, 10–12
protecting, 25
democratic decline, 10–12, 50–51
Dicey, A. V., 24
dispute resolution, 7, 44–45
dress, modes, 2
duty
to govern, 46
to protect, 46–47, 49
Dworkin, Ronald, 86
Dyzenhaus, David, 61–62

elections, 49, 64
Elkins, Zachary, 77–78
Ely, John Hart, 98–100
emergencies, 57–63
empire, age of, 20
European Convention on Human Rights (ECHR), 77, 83–86
UK Human Rights Act, and, 103–104, 106–108
executive aggrandisement, 11
executive branch
functional characteristics, 45–52
relationship with courts, 38, 72
executive power
expansion, 51

federalism, 24
Freedom House, 11
Fukuyama, Francis, 10, 12
Fuller, Lon, 41
fuzzy law, 52

Gardbaum, Stephen, 99
Ginsburg, Tom, 31, 54, 77–78, 95
Goebbels, Joseph, 16
Good Friday Agreement, 26–30
Gross, Sir Peter, 106–107

Haibronner, Michaela, 100
Hamilton, Alexander, 43, 46, 51
Hamlyn Lectures
instructions for, 10
high executive, 47–48
Hobsbawm, Eric, 5–6
Hoffmann, Lord, 29
human rights
protection of, 79–90
role of courts, 90–103
Huntington, Samuel, 11

iconography, 2
illiberalism, 53–57
impartiality, judicial, 24, 40–41
independence of judges, 43

Independent Human Rights Act Review (IHRAR) report, 107
institutional values, 35–37
International Bill of Rights, 77
International Covenant on Civil and Political Rights (ICCPR), 76
International Covenant on Economic, Social and Cultural Rights (ICESCR), 76
international human rights law, 79–80, 84–85
invented tradition, 5–6
Irvine, Lord, 104
Issacharoff, Samuel, 31

John of Salisbury, 14–15
Johnson, Boris, 15
judicial decision-making, 33
judicial reasoning, 41
judicial review, 25, 80, *See also* strong-form review; weak-form review
  political process theory of, 99–100

Kahn, Paul, 34
Kavanagh, Aileen, 92, 105–106
Korematsu v US, 61
Krygier, Martin, 4–5

Lava Jato (Car Wash) scandal, 67–68
law, 4–5, 17, *See also* fuzzy law; international human rights law
legal certainty, principle of, 40
legal culture, 35–37
legislation
  challenges to, 87–88
  determining constitutionality of, 25
limitations clauses, 86
Liversidge v Anderson, 61
Lochner v New York, 95–96
Loughlin, Martin, 8–9, 48
Lula da Silva, Luiz Inacio, 67–68
Lutz, Ellen, 66

Machiavelli, Niccolo, 58
Madison, James, 32
Mahomed, Ismail, 6
Mazower, Mark, 76
militant democracy, 26
monist/dualist divide, 84–85
Moravcsik, Andrew, 76
Moustafa, Tamir, 53–54
Mudde, Cas, 55

New Zealand Bill of Rights Act, 81
Northern Ireland Act (1998), 27–30
Northern Ireland Protocol, 30

O'Leary, Brendan, 27
Omar v Minister of Law and Order, 61
ordo-constitutionalism, 9

political process theory
  of judicial review, 99–100
politicisation, 66
populism, 55–56
Posner, Eric, 50

precedent, doctrine of, 40
proportionality test, 86
prosecutions of political actors, 65–68
public law model of adjudication, 44–45
public persona, 6

qualified rights, 85–86

reactive character of courts, 39–40
Reiger, Caitlin, 66
remedies, 88–89
Retained European Union Law (Revocation and Reform) Bill (2022), 30–31
Richardson, Sir Egerton, 76
Robinson v Secretary of State for Northern Ireland and Others, 28–29
Roman Republic, 13–14, 58
Roosevelt, Eleanor, 75
Roosevelt, Franklin D., 96
Roux, Theunis, 33–34

Sadat, Anwar, 53–54
Sadurski, Wojciech, 54
Schmitt, Carl, 58
seniority system, 2
separation of powers, 23–24
sham constitutions, 32
Shapiro, Martin, 44, 53
slowness, 42
South African Constitution, 84
Spano, Judge Robert, 108
state of exception, 58
strong-form review, 91–103

third wave of democratisation, 11
Tomkins, Adam, 45
tradition, 5
traditional model of adjudication, 44–45
Transparency International, 63–64

UK Human Rights Act, 81, 101
  debate, 103–110
UN Convention against Corruption, 65
United States v Carolene Products, 95–97
Universal Declaration of Human Rights (UDHR), 74–78, 82, 112
US Supreme Court, 8, 96

values, 35–37
Vermeule, Adrian, 50
Voigt, Stefan, 59–60

Waldron, Jeremy, 92–95, 98–99
Walters, Brian, 14
warfare, 20
weak-form review, 91, 101
written constitutions, 80
  spread, 19–21

Zondo, Raymond, 71
Zuma, Jacob, 68–72

For EU product safety concerns, contact us at Calle de José Abascal, 56–1°,
28003 Madrid, Spain or eugpsr@cambridge.org.

www.ingramcontent.com/pod-product-compliance
Lightning Source LLC
LaVergne TN
LVHW010320220926
848484LV00004BB/806
9781009545792